From the famous Boquería in Barcelona to the tiny village markets of rural Spain, market life and fresh regional products are at the heart of Spanish life and cuisine. **The Real Taste of Spain** focuses on basic ingredients and core principles to offer simple and delicious Spanish recipes.

Here are the everyday foods of Spain that are central to good home cooking: plump tomatoes, fresh fish and vegetables, ripe fruits, tasty cheeses and perfectly cured meats. With more and more of us wishing to eat a varied and healthy diet, this beautifully illustrated cookbook and reference combines this demand with Spanish food's ever-increasing popularity.

Divided by the stalls you would find in the local market: shellfish, fresh fish, charcuterie, meat, poultry and game, rice and pulses, groceries, eggs and dairy, the bakery, vegetables and fruit, each section offers delicious recipes for the type of produce on offer. Jenny Chandler brings the vitality of the market to life with introductions to each stall and explanations of the products. She also includes traditional cooking techniques and easy variations for each recipe.

With a few Spanish store-cupboard essentials and good fresh, local produce, be it from the markets of Bristol or Bilbao, you will be well on your way to re-creating the real taste of Spain.

THE REAL TASTE OF SPAIN

SPAIN

RECIPES INSPIRED BY THE MARKETS OF SPAIN

JENNY CHANDLER

PAVILION

For Peter, my rock, and our gorgeous Imogen.

This edition published in the United Kingdom in 2012 by
Pavilion Books, Old West London Magistrates Court, 10 Southcombe Street, London W14 0RA

First published in the United Kingdom in 2007 by
Pavilion Books, Old West London Magistrates Court, 10 Southcombe Street, London W14 0RA

An imprint of Anova Books Company Ltd

Senior Editor: Emily Preece-Morrison   **Designer:** Vanessa Courtier   **Recipe photography:** Vanessa Courtier
Location photography: Jenny Chandler and Peter Bassett   **Home Economy:** Jane Suthering   **Styling:** Wei Tang   **Copy Editor:** Kathy Steer

ISBN 9781862059757

A CIP catalogue record for this book is available from the British Library

10 9 8 7 6 5 4 3 2 1

Reproduction by Rival Colour, London
Printed and bound by Craft Print International Ltd, Singapore

www.anovabooks.com

Contents

introduction

The key to Spanish home cooking is its honesty. It is simply a combination of the very best basic ingredients and a little fuss-free preparation.

It is true that Spanish cuisine has evolved dramatically over the last few decades. The *Nueva Cocina* has hit international headlines and taken the restaurant world by storm. Traditional dishes are turned on their heads making dining out a roller coaster ride for the senses. *Paella* is transformed into a packet of shellfish infused Rice-Krispies while a squid ravioli might just explode in your mouth. But even Ferran Adrià, the master magician of this molecular gastronomy, insists that it is special occasion food. In fact, he goes further still, recommending that you eat at his restaurant just once in a lifetime for its spell to really work. The cutting edge *cocina* may have put Spain firmly on the Michelin map but it has done little to change the way most people eat on a daily basis.

The pace of modern life, and newly found affluence, has played much greater roles in moulding the home kitchen. Slow-cooked bean stews are increasingly replaced by a choice piece of meat or fish, ready in a matter of moments on the griddle. In the past such extravagance would have been unthinkable in much of Spain, particularly during the hungry years that followed the Civil War. But, ironically, today it is the hotpots of beans and chickpeas that come out on high days and holidays when cooks are prepared to spend their precious time slaving over a hot stove. Yet one thing has not changed, the profound appreciation for ingredients, where as much thought and importance is given to selecting the right type of rice as picking the best lobster.

Discerning home cooks and passionate gourmets still go to the market to pick up the freshest local produce on offer. Some city *mercados*, or markets such as Barcelona's Boquería or Valencia's Mercat Central are awe-inspiring buildings packed with everything from butchers and fishmongers to entire stalls of snails or wild mushrooms. Meanwhile, a weekly harbour-side market in Galicia may amount to little more than a fresh produce stall, a van from the local bakery and a fisherman selling the catch of the day. The latter certainly lacks the variety but will provide a feast all the same. What could be more delicious than a fabulously fresh, grilled sardine served with the traditional corn and rye bread? It is all down to eating what is in its prime, following seasons and regional specialities.

And so I have headed to the markets of Spain to research this book, a fascinating and enlightening experience. There were certainly days when I began to question my own sanity. One occasion, six months pregnant, scaling steep cobbled streets in 40 degrees heat only to be greeted by a sea of laced knickers and tablecloths, is memorable for all the wrong reasons. In the villages of the Alpujarras, high in the Sierra Nevada mountains, the *mercado semanal*, or weekly market, turned out to be little more than a local fruit and veg' van doing its rounds. By the time I had turned up at the fourth market running I'm sure the vendor thought that he had acquired a stalker. Yet there are so many unexpected occasions when a town square comes to life with stalls of salt cod, pungent cheeses, cured sausages and picturesque mounds of fruit and vegetables. But the most captivating part of any provincial market is the small

huddle of locals with their truly seasonal fare: a bucket of spindly wild asparagus, a biscuit tin of dried camomile, a misshapen cheese or a wheelbarrow of cherries.

The produce on offer varies enormously across the regions. A Mediterranean customer will expect an entire stand of olives, recognizing favourite varieties at a glance while a legume-lover of Asturias will carefully peruse the vast selections of dried beans before finally making his choice. Markets live and breathe the country's history too. The salted, wind-dried tuna or *mojama*, of Cádiz and Alicante is a Phoenician legacy, while the wafts of coriander and mint as you enter Malaga's bustling market through the ancient Moorish gate transport you back to the days of the Nasrid Sultans. Meanwhile, the pork, apples and cider of the North are not just results of a cooler climate but betray their Celtic heritage too.

Markets can be wonderful places to eat – late breakfast, early lunch or a snack on the hoof, there is always something on offer. A plate of warm octopus, straight from the pot, is a Galician speciality while the *churros* van does brisk trade in its doughnut fritters down south in Andalucia. Pinotxo's bar in the Boquería market is a fabulous example of the Spanish passion for honest, good food. Brothers Albert and Jordi, cook a constant stream of down-to-earth dishes on the minuscule stove behind the counter, using the best ingredients that the market has to offer. You have to move fast if you want a look in. The regular clientele of chefs, shoppers and neighbouring vendors have their names on each dish while it is still in the pan; nothing could be fresher or tastier.

The market stallholders and customers alike are a great source of recipes and tips, their enthusiasm fuelled by an immeasurable pride in their own region and produce. And, while a particular fresh pepper or peach may be impossible to find in a different area, or country for that matter, there are plenty of key ingredients that are, thankfully, widely available. The ancient Iberians had to be ingenious in their methods of preserving food to last the long harsh winters of the inland plains or stand up to the stifling heat of an August day. This necessity gave us the cured meats, salted fish, cheeses and dried pulses that are exported all over the world today. Just a pinch of smoked Spanish paprika or slither of exquisite *jamón Serrano*, or Serrano ham will immediately give your local vegetables the Iberian touch.

Ingredients are key to successful cooking, a seemingly obvious fact that is often bizarrely overlooked by many of us living in the fast lane of the western world. A tired piece of hake will never taste great, no matter how much attention you give it; you'd be better to open a can of quality tuna. So stock up your store-cupboard with a few Spanish essentials and head out to the market, be it in Bristol or Bilbao, in search of the finest produce you can get your hands on and you will be well on your way to re-creating the real taste of Spain.

marvellous mercados

Spain has dozens of fabulous food markets but here is a very subjective selection of my favourites, the unmissables, just in case you happen to be in the neighbourhood. Some are weekly affairs that bring new life and bustle to quiet backwater towns while others are fixed, municipal markets.

Fixed daily markets, open Monday–Saturday

Mercado de la Boquería (Barcelona) – Without a doubt Spain's largest and finest market. Quite apart from the incredible variety of stalls it is a fabulous place to eat breakfast or lunch. Bar Pinotxo or El Quim are my favourite spots.

Mercado de Chamartín (Madrid) – A "boutique" market if there is such a thing. An exclusive selection of the nation's finest food all under one small roof.

Mercado Central de Málaga (Andalucia) – Enter through the ancient Moorish archway into an Aladdin's cave of exotic fruit, fresh herbs and wonderful fish. And, visit the nearby Casa Aranda for some of the best *churros*, or fritters, in Spain.

Mercado de Abastos, Pontevedra (Galicia) – A seafood lover's Utopia with an incomparable selection of fish and shellfish from the Atlantic and fertile *Rías*, or estuaries.

Mercado de Abastos, Santiago de Compostela (Galicia) – A stunning setting in the old town where as well as the permanent stalls there are always dozens of locals sitting outside selling their home-grown fruit and vegetables.

Mercado Central de Valencia – A magical Art Deco building, streaming with natural light houses an incredible selection of stalls, particularly good for fruit, vegetables and seafood.

Weekly markets

Cáceres (Extremadura), Wednesdays – A small food section in the huge weekly market. It is worth a visit for a glorious selection of local sheep and goat's milk cheeses, *chorizos* and mountains of seasonal cherries.

Cangas de Ónis (Asturias), Sundays – A truly local affair with fabulous bread, cheese, cured meats and plenty of smallholders with their own fruit, vegetables, eggs and artisan cheeses.

Granollers (Catalonia), Thursdays – Arrive early to eat breakfast at the legendary Fonda de Europa. It will be packed with the all the local gents eating *Cap I Pota*, stewed calf's head and foot, but you may prefer something lighter. A great selection of live poultry, eggs, fruit and vegetables.

Gernika (Basque Country), Mondays – Plenty of fresh produce from local farmers, Sheep's cheese, peppers and beans in particular. A flourishing organic presence too.

León (Old Castille and León), Saturdays – The Plaza Mayor is transformed into a glorious food market. Large stalls of salt cod, cured meats, fruit and vegetables and plenty of locals with boxes of their own apples, walnuts or whatever the season has to offer.

Plasencia (Extremadura), Tuesdays – The bustling farmers' market has been held in the Plaza Mayor since the 12th century. Fabulous fruit and vegetables, cherry liqueur and cowbells. A huge congregation of cloth capped farmers chatting and doing business too.

Tolosa (Basque Country), Saturdays – The recently restored market has a beautiful setting on the bank of the Oria river. Local beans, peppers, sheep's cheese and wild mushrooms are the star players.

La Feria de Padrón (Galicia), Sundays – Huge baskets of the celebrated *tapas* peppers, *pimientos de Padrón* and a great selection of *chorizos*, Cow's milk cheeses and rye bread. Head for the food tents to savour some freshly cooked octopus or barbecued beef, washed down with local wine.

Annual

Fira del Gall (the Poultry Fair), Vilafranca de Penedés (Catalonia), the last weekend before Christmas – A live poultry market where punters buy their festive bird direct from producers and then hand it over to be prepared for the pot. A service offered gratis by the organizers. A great variety of poultry and an incredible display of healthy Spanish realism.

the store-cupboard

It is liberating to wander the market on the look out for the freshest piece of fish or the finest local vegetables, secure in the knowledge that all the other necessary ingredients for the feast await you back at home.

A well-stocked larder transforms both shopping and cooking into much simpler and more enjoyable tasks. You have more time, more scope for spontaneity, and throwing together pre-dinner nibbles or a last minute supper is never a problem.

This small selection of key, non-perishable ingredients will bring the true flavour of Spain to your table.

Alcohol

White and red wine should always be at your disposal. Extremely complex, expensive wines are wasted in the pot but a cheap bottle of paint stripper can ruin a dish too. The oxidized dregs from last month's dinner party just won't do.

Sherry gives a wonderful depth of flavour to many dishes and contrary to popular belief does not keep ad infinitum once opened; a perfect excuse to have a tipple yourself, while you do the cooking. *Vi Ranci* is an oxidized, sweet white wine used in the Catalan kitchen, but a sweet sherry can be substituted.

Brandy and *anis*, or aniseed liqueur are used in both savoury and sweet dishes.

Fish and shellfish

Canned clams and mussels make excellent instant nibbles to enjoy with a glass of wine or sherry.

Salted anchovies are sometimes used in sauces or salads, but are most often enjoyed with a drink. The best are from Cantabria and Catalonia. I adore the *boquerones en vinagre*, the vinegar pickled anchovies, available in vacuum packs.

Canned tuna, especially the premium *bonito del norte*, albacore, is a wonderful salad standby.

Salt cod, or *bacalao,* is sometimes tricky to come by outside Spain, so it is worth snapping up when you can get it (see page 44). Keep it somewhere cool, dry and preferably airtight unless you fancy the entire cupboard smelling of fish.

Fruit

Dried apricots, figs, prunes and sultanas are often used in delicious combinations with poultry, meat and game. They also make popular accompaniments to cheese. Look out for the plump raisins from Málaga – heaven soaked overnight in brandy or sweet sherry and served with ice cream.

Pulses

A selection of dried chickpeas, lentils and beans is vital for good hearty stews and soups (see pages 86–99), but do keep a fast turnover as all legumes eventually go stale. It is also an idea to keep some of the good-quality jars of ready cooked *judiones,* or butter beans or chickpeas for quick last minute suppers.

Nuts

Nuts are best bought whole and raw, then roasted or ground when needed (see page 108).

Almonds are the most ubiquitous Spanish nuts, nibbled with drinks, and also a key ingredient in numerous sweet and savoury dishes. Look out for delicious Marcona almonds.

Hazelnuts, walnuts and pine kernels should be bought in small quantities and used quickly before they turn rancid and stale.

Olives and capers

Olives make the perfect accompaniment to a drink and keep very well in brine or olive oil. Green olives, such as the *manzanilla* or *gordal* are the most popular table olives in Spain, often stuffed with anchovies or peppers. Tiny purple *arbequina* olives from Catalonia are fabulous too.

Capers are useful for salads and sauces. The larger caperberries are wonderful with cured meats or served with a selection of *tapas*.

Olive oil

The Spanish produce and use more olive oil than any other country in the world. The cold-pressed *Aceite de Virgen Extra* is usually reserved for salads, dipping bread into, or drizzling on cooked dishes where its complex flavours can be appreciated. There are dozens of top quality extra virgin olive oils on offer, many with their own *Denominación de Origen* (DO) [see page 16].

The flavour can vary enormously from green, grassy oils from the early harvest through to the fruitier, golden oils made with the riper olives. Climate, soil and the type of olive will all affect the end result too. It is all a question of personal taste, just as you may prefer one wine to another. My personal favourites, at the moment are from the Baena DO in Andalucia and the Siurana DO in Catalonia.

The milder, second pressing oil, referred to purely as *Aceite de Oliva,* is used for cooking and frying. The oil should be kept somewhere cool and dark and used within 6 months of opening.

Peppers

Canned and bottled peppers are useful for salads and as tasty garnishes for cooked dishes.

Guindillas Vascas are pickled green chilli peppers. They range from sharp and sweet varieties to the seriously fiery numbers that add a fabulous punch to a bowl of beans (see page 91).

Pimientos del Bierzo Asados are a particularly good type of roasted and peeled capsicum peppers.

Pimientos de Piquillo (see page 107) have a more piquant flavour. They may seem expensive but a small 220 g/8 oz can will yield about 16 peppers, roasted, peeled and ready for stuffing.

Dried *ñoras* peppers and *choricero* peppers look beautiful hanging in the kitchen and will keep well for a few months. They give an authentic flavour to many sauces and stews. Paprika makes a good substitute when they are not available.

Cured pork

Salchichón, longaniza or the Catalan *fuet* are firm, cured pork sausages (see pages 48–9). They are deliciously chewy and a great treat to offer with drinks or to keep hunger at bay while preparing a meal. Remove the skin before slicing, as it has a horrible habit of getting caught between the back teeth.

Chorizo (see page 49) is ideal for flavouring stews and bean dishes or cooking with a little wine or cider for a quick snack (see page 54). Vacuum packed soft semi-cured *chorizo* will keep for a few weeks in the refrigerator while the harder, fully cured variety will keep for up to a year in a cool, dry place.

Jamón (see pages 48–9) is best sliced just before eating as it can dry out but can be purchased in vacuum packs. I like to have a couple of small packs of the chopped pieces, the size of French *lardons* (diced bacon), in store ready for cooked dishes.

Rice

The Levante, or eastern regions of Spain consume huge quantities of rice. The vast proportion is short-grain rice used for *paellas* and soupier *arroz* dishes. La Bomba rice is the most reliable, and needless to say, expensive variety on offer. Long-grain rice is also used for some salads and supper dishes.

Spices

Paprika, ground dried pepper or *pimentón* is the most extensively used spice. It ranges from the sweet, *dulce*, through sweet and sour, *agridulce* to the hot, *picante*. *Pimentón* from the Murcia in the east is traditionally sun-dried while the paprika from Extremadura, *De La Vera* in particular, is smoked over oak. It is wise to have some of each in store.

Saffron, the world's most costly spice, is best purchased in small quantities as whole strands (stigmas) rather than ground. It gives colour and earthy flavour to many stews, particularly rice dishes.

Cinnamon, cumin and aniseed are best bought as sticks or whole seeds, being ground as and when required.

Tomate frito

Tomate frito is a simple sauce of sieved fried tomatoes with olive oil sold by the can or jar. Some varieties can be rather too sweet but a good-quality version makes a quick option to throw in with beans or over rice.

Vinegar

Wine vinegar is used in many sauces and *escabeches*, or pickles. White wine vinegar sits on the table alongside olive oil, allowing individuals to dress their own salad.

Vinagre de Jerez, sherry vinegar, is aged in the sherry barrels giving it an unbelievable depth of warm, intense flavour. It is delicious added to *Gazpacho* (see page 150) and salads.

a stamp of quality – the *Denominación de Origen*

The *Denomición de Origen* (DO) or literally designation of origin, is a regulatory system set up by the Spanish Ministry of Agriculture, Fisheries and Food. It works like the French *Appellation* system but in the Spanish case it stretches to dozens of products and not just to wine.

When you buy a cheese, an extra virgin olive oil, cured meat or wine from a DO you are guaranteed a certain quality. The ingredients and the entire production process, as well as the geographical origin of each product have been subject to strict regulations. And there are quite literally dozens of foodstuffs with their own DO to look out for, from cheese to chickpeas, from peppers to pork.

DO products are easily identified, wearing their badge with obvious pride. They are definitely worth tracking down, particularly when you are in unfamiliar territory. Saffron, for instance, is a justifiably expensive spice, requiring well over a hundred crocus flowers to produce just one gram of the precious dried stigmas. But how can you be confident that you are buying the good stuff with its characteristic toasty flavour or in fact, that you are buying saffron at all? Well that is where the assurance of a DO label is invaluable.

Yet there is nothing to say that a classified vinegar, honey or any product for that matter, should necessarily be superior to its unregulated neighbour. DO produce often comes with a high price tag to match its status and a local supplier may well be able to introduce you to a bargain alternative blessed with equal virtues.

what to drink?

Spain has more land under vines than any other country in the world and so it will come as no surprise that wine and water accompany virtually every meal. Beer may be consumed in ever-increasing quantities in the *tapas* bar but when it comes to eating, nothing can begin to compare with the marriage of food and wine. Even children are allowed a splash of wine at the meal, often watered down with *gaseosa*, or lemonade.

I shall make no attempt to give an all encompassing view on such a vast subject, there are after all over one hundred recognized wine regions to deal with. But, here are a few pointers when it comes to selecting a Spanish wine.

The DO system (see above) becomes a little more complicated where wine is concerned. A DO wine will be a mainstream, quality wine while a DOC is considered the next step up the ladder in both price and quality.

Spain has always been known for its red wines, those from Rioja in particular, but nowadays there is plenty of competition. Extremely fine reds with international reputations to match are now produced in Ribera del Duero, Navarra and Priorato. Huge investment and modern techniques are bringing more and more areas into the picture too. Valdepeñas and Jumilla may be the places to look for bargains today, but it is wise to seek the advice of a good wine merchant.

When it comes to white wine the crisp Albariños of the Galician Rias Baixas are fabulous with seafood. Even the regions of Rueda and Rioja that used to produce some pretty flabby, oaky styles have taken on a new lease of life producing more contemporary, deliciously fresh styles. The ever-popular *Cava* of Penedés, Spain's answer to Champagne, deserves a mention too – an ideal glass of fizz for a celebration.

But my personal favourites are those wines so unique to Spain – the sherries. I am amazed by the number of wine lovers who have yet to succumb to the charms of sherry. And, if you think it is an aperitif reserved for the 'twin-set and pearls' brigade, then think again.

From the chilled dry *Finos* and *Manzanillas* that taste divine with olives, almonds and a myriad of *tapas* to the raisiny depths of a sweet *Pedro Jiménez*, there is a sherry for every occasion. Nutty *Amontillados* match seafood beautifully while *Olorosos* make a fabulous match for cheese. Small, half bottles of sherry are an excellent idea, since contrary to popular belief sherry does go off, particularly the dry unoxidized styles of *Fino* and *Manzanilla*. I would also not recommend consuming sherry in too large a quantity. Many years ago I spent a night on the tiles in San Lúcar de Barrameda drinking the local *Manzanilla*. I had been swept up in the revelry and excitement that precedes the annual *Romería del Rocío*, a spectacular pilgrimage in the Virgin de Rocío's honour, and hell, did I pay for it the next day!

useful utensils

The traditional Spanish kitchen is devoid of much specialist gadgetry but there are a few bits and pieces that could certainly help you to cook like a local.

Cazuelas are fabulously useful, terracotta cooking pots with straight, low sides. They come in all sizes: from huge vessels big enough to feed the entire family down to individual *tapas* dishes. The tiny 4 cm/1½ inch diameter versions are perfect for *Crema Catalana* (see page 119). This all-purpose earthenware can be used for gentle frying over a gas flame, for roasting in a hot oven and even looks attractive enough to serve at the table.

Always 'cure' a *cazuela* before using it for the first time. Soak it in water for a few hours and then place it in the oven filled with water for 10 minutes.

A heat diffuser, to set over your stove, can be very useful as many dishes are simmered slowly on the top of the hob. You can, of course, place them in a low oven instead, if you prefer.

The mortar and pestle are essential in the traditional kitchen. Most are ceramic bowls with a wooden pestle, but stone versions also work well. The mortar must be large enough not just for crushing spices but for mixing sauces and seasonings too, at least 15 cm/6 inches in diameter. Modern cooks often use a blender

instead but purists will tell you that the texture and flavour is never the same.

A small, deep omelette pan is key to the perfect *tortilla*. A 20 cm/8 inch, non-stick pan with deep sides will make a juicy five-egg omelette.

A paella pan, or very large frying pan is a must for successful *paellas* (see pages 97–8). A 40 cm/16 inch base will feed 6–8 people. Pans are usually made from light steel and should be oiled slightly before storing or they will rust, rather like a wok.

The *pasapurés* is a rotary sieve that performs the same job as a food processor while simultaneously straining out bones, skins and pips. It is fabulous for preparing soups, purées, jams and jellies. It is often known by its French name, the *mouli-legumes*.

Small metal moulds are ideal for preparing individual puddings such as *Flan*, *Crème Caramel*, or serving moulded portions of rice – 200 ml/7 fl oz is the ideal size.

shellfish

The shellfish stall, or *parada de mariscos*, is invariably the most arresting sight in the Spanish market. The sheer volume and variety of crustaceans and molluscs on offer is mind-boggling. It is also, without a doubt, where the most cash changes hands too. The Spanish have an insatiable appetite for seafood and are prepared to pay exorbitant prices to satisfy their craving. Prices soar before every festival and bank holiday, and there are plenty of those, while the Christmas season often sees prices double. So, despite the fact that Spain lands vast quantities of shellfish on her lengthy shorelines, do not expect a bargain. In fact, demand often far outstrips supply. It is not uncommon to see crates of tiny blue swimmer crabs from Scottish waters or mounds of Irish *cigalas*, or Dublin Bay Prawns, beside the local catch. Yet, of one thing you can be certain: the best variety and quality of shellfish

you will find anywhere in Europe; the locals are discerning customers.

A trip to the shellfish stalls in Barcelona's Boquería market is an unforgettable experience. Assistants with immaculate hair styles and scarlet lips nudge the live crustaceans as you pass, causing a shock wave of clattering claws across the piles of crushed ice. There are delicacies from every corner of Spain: spiny lobsters, spider crabs, deep red *carabinero* prawns and translucent grey shrimp, bundles of razor clams and nets of mussels. You name it, it's here. So where does one begin? Well, it would seem that the locals are as indecisive as the rest of us and many of the traditional dishes include half a dozen different species in the same pot, or *paella*.

The *lonjas*, or wholesale markets, on the coast are well worth a visit. The quayside at Pálamos on the

Costa Brava comes to life in the late afternoon. Crate upon crate of the legendary local prawns are hauled into the saleroom, auctioned and then whisked away by the awaiting fleet of refrigerated vans, all in a matter of minutes. Thankfully there are a handful of small traders who sell to the public too. A few stunningly fresh *gambas a la plancha*, or griddled prawns, are my idea of heaven, you can keep your lobster any day. In fact, nothing can beat tucking into the local speciality in situ: freshly shucked oysters on Vigo's Ria de la Pescadería or sweet pilgrim scallops on the dockside in Finisterre. Galicia certainly does top the menu when it comes to shellfish. The shallow Western *rias*, or estuaries, make fertile beds for oysters, scallops, clams and mussels. And the local market at Pontevedra is a mind-blowing spectacle with over 200 stands of gloriously fresh seafood.

The Spanish are adventurous consumers too. Cauldron's of octopus bubble away at Galician country markets providing shoppers with a quick snack, a far cry from the ubiquitous hot dog. Raw sea urchin coral is an Asturian treat while the Basques love to prise periwinkles from their shells with a pin. Tiny bundles of sea slug fillets, known rather perplexingly as *espardenyes*, or *espadrilles*, are a delicacy in Catalonia. But the *percebe*, or goose-necked barnacle, tops the bill. This tubular creature clings to the roughest stretches of the northern coastline, and the collectors famously risk life and limb to snatch their rare prize from amidst dashing Atlantic breakers. The orange flesh that is sucked from the centre of the barely cooked barnacle is a pure taste of the sea, exquisite in its subtlety. And so it is, that a bizarre crustacean resembling a reptilian toe can fetch up to 180 Euros a kilo.

gambas pil pil
sizzling garlic prawns

A tapas bar classic all over Southern Spain: the prawns are a solo act so they must be the freshest you can buy. This is a last minute dish that should sizzle its way to the table. It is best cooked in a small, ovenproof terracotta *cazuela*, which is also ideal for serving. Take great care not to burn the garlic or the entire dish will be bitter. Some crusty white bread dipped in the garlickly oil is sublime.

serves 4

6 tbsp olive oil
3 garlic cloves, thinly sliced
2–3 small dried chillies,
  finely chopped

500 g/1 lb 2 oz fresh prawns,
  peeled with tails left intact
pinch of salt
pinch of sweet paprika

Heat the olive oil in a small, ovenproof terracotta *cazuela*, or frying pan over a high heat. Add the garlic and chillies and cook for a matter of seconds until you can smell the heady wafts of garlic.

Add the prawns and cook until just pink and firm. Sprinkle with salt and paprika and serve quickly so that the prawns are still sizzling in the cooking juices.

Variation   You may like to add a tablespoon of dry sherry together with the prawns and garnish the dish with chopped parsley.

Know your shrimps and prawns

Camarones are tiny shrimps, which turn white when cooked and are eaten shell and all. In Cádiz they are cooked in delicious fritters, *tortillitas*.

Quisquillas are small brown shrimp, which are often added to the popular scrambled egg dish, *revuelto*.

Gambas are transparent prawns that turn a stunning pink when cooked. They are fabulous cooked *a la plancha*, or on the griddle, or *pil pil* style.

Carabineros are large tasty prawns with dramatic red shells even when raw.

Langostinos are the huge, over 20 cm/8 inch, striped prawns often known as tiger prawns.

Making prawn stock

Never throw away raw prawn shells or heads, they make wonderful stock, which is a great base for any seafood dish. Place them in a large pan and cover with cold water. Bring to the boil, then reduce the heat slightly and simmer gently for 20 minutes. Strain the stock into a bowl. I like to squeeze absolutely all the juices from the heads and shells in the sieve using the bottom of a ladle. This gives a cloudy but wonderful stock. You could add onion, carrot, parsley stalks, peppercorns or slices of lemon to the pan for extra flavour.

almejas a la marinera
clams a la marinera

The ground floor of Pontevedra's market is almost entirely devoted to seafood, with the half dozen butchers' stalls destined to play second fiddle on the sidelines. This is Spain's shellfish capital with a spectacular selection of crab, lobster, scallops and, of course, the mussels and clams that are farmed in the shallow, warm waters of the *rías*, or estuaries, that punctuate Galicia's west coast.

Among the wide variety of clams on offer is the highly prized *almeja fina*, or carpet shell clam. It also goes by the name of *almeja de Carril* and when you visit the nearby harbour of Carril it is easy to see why. The waters are a forest of stakes, each post marking the boundary of an individual clam bed, a highly productive business passed down among the locals from generation to generation.

Buying and cleaning clams

Only buy clams, and mussels, if most of their shells are closed. Lots of open shells indicate that they are not very fresh. Tap any open shell before cooking, and if it does not close discard it. The animal is dead and could cause food poisoning.

If you want to buy clams, or mussels, ahead of time then place them in a very cool larder or your refrigerator covered with a damp cloth.

Clams can sometimes be very sandy, so it's worth soaking them in salt water for a few hours to sluice them of any grit. Some people add breadcrumbs or oatmeal too to help the process.

serves 4

3 tbsp olive oil
4 garlic cloves, finely diced
1 small onion, finely diced
1 small dried chilli, left whole
2 tbsp plain flour
1.5 kg/3¼ lb fresh clams, ideally almejas finas, cleaned (see right)

1 tbsp finely chopped fresh flat-leaf parsley
50 ml/2 fl oz *fino* sherry or dry white wine
50 ml/2 fl oz water or fish stock
fresh white bread, to serve

Heat the olive oil in a large pan with a tight-fitting lid, add the garlic, onion and chilli and fry gently until the onion is soft and transparent. Sprinkle over the flour and stir for a moment or two.

Next add the clams together with the parsley, sherry or wine and water or fish stock. Cover with the lid and increase the heat and cook, checking every couple of minutes and stirring, until the clams have opened, leaving the flesh lusciously juicy. Discard any clams that are still closed after cooking.

Serve at once with plenty of white bread to soak up the delicious sauce.

Variations   Try adding a little finely chopped *jamón Serrano* with the garlic and onion.

Cook this recipe with mussels, but because the mussel shells are lighter you will only need 900 g/2 lb to serve 4. They will also cook more quickly, so keep a watchful eye on them: overcooked shellfish is tough and rubbery.

mejillones gratinados
grilled mussels

Spain is the world's leading producer of mussels. At first glance the *rias*, or estuaries, of western Galicia seem to be packed with sinister fleets of battleships that, on closer inspection, turn out to be hundreds of small rafts. Huge, lusciously tender mussels grow on ropes suspended from these rafts. This highly productive farming makes them an absolute bargain in comparison with other, more elusive, shellfish. Another advantage of rope-grown mussels is that they don't contain grit like their wild cousins that live on the seashore, which are constantly washed by the sandy tide.

serves 4

- 1 kg/2 ¼ lb fresh mussels, cleaned and steamed
- 4 tbsp olive oil
- 1 onion, finely diced
- 1 red pepper, finely diced
- 85 g/3¼ oz unsmoked bacon, finely chopped
- 3 garlic cloves, crushed
- 2 tbsp tomato purée
- 2 tbsp fresh parsley, finely chopped
- 5 tbsp breadcrumbs
- 2 tbsp extra virgin olive oil

Remove the 'lids' from the mussels, leaving them on the half shell. Place them in a large, shallow ovenproof dish and set aside.

Heat the olive oil in a pan, add the onion, red pepper and bacon and fry until they begin to colour. Add the garlic and cook, stirring, until you catch its fantastic aroma. Add the tomato purée and turn off the heat.

Mix the parsley, breadcrumbs and extra virgin olive oil together in a bowl.

Preheat your grill to medium. No grill? An extremely hot oven will do. Next spoon the onion mixture over the mussels and top with the breadcrumbs.

Place under the grill until the mussels are sizzling hot and the breadcrumbs are crisp and browned.

Tip You can partially pre-prepare this dish. Steam the mussels and set them in their baking dish, cover with clingfilm and **make sure** to refrigerate them until you are ready to use. Prepare the sauce and, **once cooled**, spoon over the mussels and refrigerate. Top with the breadcrumbs and place under the grill at the last moment.

Variation You may like to spice up the sauce with a pinch of hot paprika or a couple of tiny dried chillies.

Preparing and steaming mussels
Ensure that all the mussels are closed before cooking. Any open mussels should be given a sharp tap, if they remain open then discard them. Don't take any chances; they could cause bad food poisoning.

Scrub the shells and remove any hairy 'beards'.

Add a few tablespoons of wine or water to a large saucepan with a lid and add the mussels. Cover and place over a high heat for about 3–4 minutes. As soon as all the mussels have opened they are ready. Discard any that remain closed.

The cooking liquid makes a fabulous stock base if it is not used immediately in the recipe, just be sure to strain away any grit if you are using wild mussels.

vieras a la gallega
galician scallops

The scallop shell has great significance across northern Europe; it is the symbol of Galicia's Santiago de Compostela, where the shrine of St James has drawn penitent pilgrims from the far reaches of Christendom for over a thousand years.

Scallops are still a common treat in Santiago, simply baked in their shells with a little wine, parsley and garlic. I particularly like this version with a touch of salty *jamón* that serves to emphasize the natural sweetness of the scallop.

serves 4

4 tbsp olive oil, plus extra for
  oiling
A small, hazelnut-sized knob of
  butter
1 onion, finely diced
4 garlic cloves, crushed
85 g/3¼ oz thick slice of *jamón
  Serrano*, diced

100 ml/3½ fl oz dry white wine
2 tbsp breadcrumbs
1 large sprig of fresh parsley,
  chopped
salt
8 large or 12 medium scallops,
  shucked and prepared (see right)

Preheat the oven to 230°C/450°F/Gas Mark 8.

Heat 2 tbsp of the olive oil and the butter in a pan, add the onion and fry until it is soft and translucent. Next add the garlic and the *jamón*, do not remove any fat, this will render and add to the flavour of the sauce. Once the garlic has begun to colour pour in the wine, increase the heat to high and cook until the liquid is reduced by half.

Meanwhile, oil 4 scallop shells, individual terracotta *cazuelas*, or gratin dishes with a little bit of olive oil and put into the oven to heat through.

Next pour the remaining olive oil into a bowl, add the breadcrumbs, parsley and a pinch of salt and mix together.

Place the scallops, with their orange roe, in the preheated dishes. Pour over the sauce, top with the breadcrumbs and bake in the oven for 5–10 minutes until the scallops are just opaque. Serve at once.

Tip   If you are entertaining, you could prepare the sauce and breadcrumbs ahead of time and then throw everything together at the last moment.

Buying scallops

Ideally buy scallops in their shells because these will not have been 'soaked', a process using tripolyphosphate by which scallops are plumped with extra moisture. 'Soaked' scallops are often not as fresh as their 'dry' counterparts and tend to boil in their own juices rather than sear. Many frozen scallops have been 'soaked'.

Ask your fishmonger to remove the scallops from their shells.

If you are buying ready-shucked scallops the white abductor muscle, the scallop meat, should have a creamy tinge rather than the white glow of a soap commercial, which belies the use of phosphates.

Try to find the premium priced, hand-harvested diver scallops, they are less muddy and kinder to the sea bed than the dredged variety.

Preparing scallops

Remove the thick white membrane around the outside of the scallop meat as well as the small tough muscle opposite the coral. If the scallops are really large you may cut them in half horizontally when searing or frying.

Be extremely careful not to overcook scallops as they will lose their melt in the mouth sweetness, becoming tough and rubbery.

pulpo a la gallega
galician octopus

Market day in Ribadavia was particularly dank; even the locals scuttled around looking miserable under their umbrellas and they are used to the damp. This southerly Galician town is often shrouded in the thick mist that floods up the Miño river valley from the Atlantic. A small crowd huddled around the *pulpería*, or octopus stall, Galicia's answer to the hot dog van, waiting for the first round of tender tentacles. A lady snipped up the freshly cooked flesh with scissors while her ruddy cheeked accomplice began dunking the next octopus in and out of a huge copper cauldron of water. The small wooden plate of warm *pulpo* dressed with olive oil and paprika and washed down with a glass of the local Ribiero wine was a welcome antidote to the drizzle.

serves 4

½ onion, left in 1 piece
2 bay leaves
1 cleaned and 'tenderized'
   octopus, weighing about
   1–1.8 kg/2–4 lb (see right)

2 tbsp extra virgin olive oil
salt
1 tsp sweet paprika and a pinch of
   hot paprika

Place the onion and bay leaves in a very large saucepan, fill it with water and bring it to the boil. Once boiling hard, 'shock' the octopus by dipping it in and out of the water 3 or 4 times with a pair of tongs until the tentacles begin to curl. This will keep the skin intact and give a deliciously tender result.

Reduce the heat slightly to a good simmer and continue to cook for about 30–45 minutes, or until a skewer slides easily through the flesh. Remove from the heat and leave the octopus to rest for 10 minutes.

Cut the tentacles into thick slices, the locals use a pair of scissors for the job, and pile them onto a wooden board or plate. Drizzle with extra virgin olive oil and sprinkle with salt and paprika.

Tuck in with a cocktail stick while the octopus is still warm.

Tip   The cooked octopus can be covered and kept for a couple of days in the refrigerator, just make sure you let it come back to room temperature and add the seasoning at the last minute.

Any leftovers would be delicious in a typical *empanada* (see page 130).

Cleaning and tenderizing octopus

To clean the octopus, begin by turning back the tentacles, revealing the mouth and beak. Remove the beak and cut away the muscles that hold the innards inside the head. You can now turn the head inside out and remove any entrails before washing thoroughly. Give the suckers a good wash too to remove any stubborn sand.

Tenderizing an octopus is a much easier job than you might imagine. You can forget all those tales of a half-hour pounding the fresh octopus on the rocky shoreline or thrashing it around in the washing machine or even a cement mixer, which you just happen to have to hand, 48 hours in the freezer will do the trick.

salpicón de mariscos
shellfish vinaigrette ·

Here is a truly refreshing mixture, a treat when shellfish is fabulously fresh and sweet. You can play around with the recipe according to what is at its best, any selection of lobster, crab, prawns, shrimps, octopus, squid, baby cuttlefish, clams or mussels will be delicious. The absolute key to this dish is not to overcook the fish. You will need to begin a few hours in advance.

serves 4–6 as a starter

salt
½ lemon, sliced
1 onion, quartered
1 bay leaf
A few fresh parsley stalks
5 black peppercorns
700 g/1½ lb prawns, with shells left on
700 g/1½ lb squid, cleaned and cut into rings (see page 28), leaving tentacles whole if small enough

500 g/1 lb 2 oz fresh mussels, cleaned, steamed and removed from their shells (see page 22)

for the vinaigrette
1 green pepper, very finely diced (think kaleidoscope)
2 tomatoes, peeled and finely diced
2 tbsp capers, rinsed and drained
2 tbsp onion, very finely diced
1 tbsp chopped fresh parsley

Begin by boiling a large saucepan of salted water with the lemon quarters, onion, bay leaf, parsley stalks and peppercorns. Drop in the prawns and once the water has come back up to the boil, cook for 1 minute. Remove the prawns with a slotted spoon and cool under cold running water.

Peel the prawns, reserving the heads and shells for stock (see page 20). Remove the black thread that runs down their back with a sharp knife as it can be rather gritty, then cut in half lengthways.

Next, using the same water in the pan, bring it back to the boil and quite literally dunk in the squid rings and tentacles until they turn opaque, a matter of seconds. Any longer and you will end up with rubber bands. Leave to cool.

Mix together all the ingredients for the vinaigrette in a bowl large enough to hold your shellfish. Add the prawns, squid and mussels and stir well. Place in the refrigerator for at least 6 hours or overnight, stirring from time to time.

Serve chilled.

calamares a la romana
fried squid

A heavenly way to eat squid, if it is prepared right. These melt in the mouth squid rings bear absolutely no resemblance to the rubber bands in greasy batter served at many a beach bar on the Costas.

serves 4 as a starter or tapas

1 kg/2¼ lb squid, cleaned, bodies cut into 2 cm/¾ inch rings, tentacles reserved for later use
150 g/5 oz plain flour
1 tsp salt

olive or vegetable oil, for frying
1 lemon, cut into segments
***Allioli* (see page 114), to serve (optional)**

Dry off the squid rings with a little kitchen paper.

Place the flour on a large plate and sprinkle with the salt. Add the squid rings and toss until coated.

Heat enough oil for frying in a deep saucepan or deep-fat fryer until a bread cube browns in about 30 seconds (see page 81). Add the squid in batches, too much at a time will lower the heat of the oil and the squid must cook quickly or they will become tough and chewy. As soon as the squid are golden remove with a slotted spoon and leave to drain on kitchen paper.

Once all the squid is cooked serve immediately garnished with the lemon segments, preferably with a bowl of *Allioli* to dip into.

Cleaning squid
Hold the squid in one hand and pull on the tentacles with the other. Set the empty body aside and deal first with the tentacles, head, silvery ink sack and innards.

Cut the tentacles off just below the eyes. Remove the tough little beak right in the centre of the tentacles; it will pop out if you push your finger through the middle. Remove the ink sac from the innards, if using, taking care not to puncture it.

Now back to the body. Scrape the membrane from the body and pull off the fins; these can be used too. Pull out the cartilage or 'quill' from the body then wash thoroughly leaving you with a white, empty tube, which is perfect for stuffing.

calamares en su tinta
squid in ink sauce

A plate of jet-black squid, however delicious, can be an alarming sight for the uninitiated. I experienced one dish so thick with ink that I was instantly transformed into a Halloween hag with a mouthful of stained teeth: just the thing for an evening out on a hot date!

This traditional recipe from Cantabria in the North dilutes the ink a little with a sauce of tomatoes and red wine.

Buying and storing cephalopods
All cephalopods, octopus, cuttlefish and squid, should smell sweet and fresh with no hint of ammonia. They freeze well, in fact octopus becomes more tender with at least 48 hours freezing. If you are not using them straight away remove the innards from squid and cuttlefish.

Ink imparts extra flavour, along with a dramatic look, to many squid and cuttlefish dishes. Cuttlefish ink is more plentiful and also reputedly sweeter than squid ink and is available in small sachets from delicatessens and fishmongers.

serves 4

- 1 kg/2¼ lb small squid, cleaned and prepared (see opposite) with ink sacs
- 3 tbsp olive oil
- 2 onions, finely chopped
- 2 garlic cloves, crushed
- 2 tbsp finely chopped fresh parsley
- 2 tbsp breadcrumbs
- 3 tbsp plain flour
- 1 tsp hot non-smoked paprika
- 300 ml/10 fl oz fish or chicken stock
- 2 ripe tomatoes, grated (see page 152)
- 1 bay leaf
- 1 sachet of cuttlefish ink (optional)
- 150 ml/5 fl oz red wine
- salt and freshly ground black pepper
- freshly cooked white rice or bread, to serve

Chop the tentacles and wings of the squid into pieces.

Heat 1 tbsp olive oil in a pan, add half of the onions and fry until soft and transparent. Next, add half of the garlic and the tentacles and cook until you can smell the garlic. Add half of the parsley and the breadcrumbs.

Use this mixture to stuff the squid bodies. Take care not to overfill them or they will split during cooking. Seal each body with a cocktail stick.

Place the flour on a plate, add the squid and toss until coated. Heat the remaining olive oil in a large frying pan and fry the squid until lightly browned. Set aside.

Now, using the same pan, fry the remaining onion until transparent. Add the remaining garlic and the paprika and stir for a minute. Pour in the stock, tomatoes and bay leaf and simmer.

Meanwhile, place the ink sacs in a sieve over a bowl and break them open with a spoon. Pour over the wine, working it through the sacs with the spoon. Repeat this process 2 or 3 times.

Add the ink and wine mixture to the sauce together with the squid and season with salt and pepper to taste. Cover the pan and simmer over a low heat for 45 minutes.

Garnish with the remaining parsley and serve with white rice or bread.

Variation You could add two slices of *jamón Serrano*, finely chopped, with the stuffing.

zarzuela
seafood 'operetta'

The seafood stands in Barcelona's Boquería market are a shellfish showcase. With so many varieties of crustacean on offer choosing can be a mind-boggling experience. This recipe solves the problem, just take a little of everything you fancy. Feel free to direct your own Operetta: the seafood can be varied according to what is available on the day, your personal taste and budget.

serves 4

2 tbsp plain flour
1 tsp salt
400–600 g/14–1¼ lb hake, cut into 4 steaks (cod or halibut would be wonderful too)
400–600 g/14–1¼ lb monkfish, cut into 4 steaks
150 ml/5 fl oz olive oil
12 prawns, shells left on
4 langoustine/Dublin bay prawns, or *cigalas*
1 medium onion, finely chopped
2 garlic cloves, crushed
2 tbsp Spanish brandy
1 dried chilli, left whole

2 large tomatoes, peeled and chopped
1 bay leaf
1 tsp sweet paprika
few saffron strands
2 tbsp chopped fresh parsley
200 ml/7 fl oz dry white wine
200 ml/7 fl oz fish stock (see page 34)
1 large squid, cleaned and cut into 4 pieces
8 fresh clams, cleaned (see page 21)
8 fresh mussels, cleaned (see page 22)
crusty bread, to serve

Mix the flour and salt together on a large plate, add the fish and toss until coated. Shake off any excess flour.

Heat the olive oil in a large frying pan or shallow casserole, add the fish and fry until there is a little colour on both sides. You are browning rather than cooking it through at this stage. Set aside once golden.

Add the prawns and langoustine to the pan and fry until just pink, then set aside too. Now, using the same oil, fry the onion until translucent, then add the garlic and cook for another couple of minutes.

Pour on the brandy and shake the pan over the heat until it flames. Once the alcohol has burned off add the chilli, tomatoes, bay leaf, paprika, saffron and most of the parsley and cook for 5 minutes, stirring from time to time.

Pour in the wine and fish stock and simmer for a further 5 minutes. Add all the reserved seafood together with the squid, mussels and clams. Cover the pan. If you don't have a lid a baking sheet will do and continue to simmer for about 8–10 minutes until the mussels and clams have opened.

Using a slotted spoon, remove the bay leaf and chilli. Sprinkle with the remaining parsley and serve at once with some good crusty bread.

fish

The fact that Spain, with its extensive Atlantic, Biscay and Mediterranean coastlines consumes more fish per capita than any other nation in Europe is not particularly surprising. What is astonishing is that Europe's largest wholesale fish market should be found in Madrid, over 300 km from the coast.

The *Madrileños* are obsessed with their fish and so, every dawn scores of white vans hurtle inland with their catch. The biggest, the freshest, the most highly sought after; it all invariably ends up in the capital to be snapped up by restaurant chefs and a few upmarket fishmongers. Ernesto Prieto's legendary stand in the smart Mercado Chamartín is a showcase of the nation's most highly prized and, quite possibly, most highly priced fish and shellfish. Chefs, gastronomes and well-heeled housewives can be sure of exceptional quality as they patiently wait their turn. Turbot, sea bass, hake and monkfish,

the selection is outstanding and there are the choicest cuts too. Here you can find elusive *kokotxas*, little morsels of gelatinous flesh from the hake's throat, worshipped in the Basque country or the *ventresca de atún*, the tuna's most succulent meat, from the belly.

Meanwhile, on the Mediterranean coast near Tarragona fishermen's wives set up their trestle tables on the dockside. The commercial fish auction takes place in the nearby *lonja*, or wholesale market, but these ladies are selling off the scraps. On offer is a motley-looking selection of tiny rockfish, scarlet scorpion fish and other bony specimens. Locals snap them up to make the deliciously rich stock that flavours traditional rice dishes such as *arròs a banda* or *paella*. In the right hands, these are every bit as good as a prime hake steak, at a fraction of the price.

Coastal markets such as Galicia's Pontevedra or Barcelona's Bouquería are the jewels in the crown when it comes to seasonal, local fish. Spotted rays, monkfish, red mullet, huge grouper, or the majestic gilt-head sea bream; there will always be something to take your fancy. Smaller markets have their magic too. In Málaga an old guy sat on an orange box painstakingly filleting tiny fresh anchovies, ready for frying or pickling in vinegar. Land bound Trujillo, in the depths of Extremadura, was hardly a promising prospect and yet I came across a local passion for tench, and a very tasty fish it proved to be. And then there was my *Sevillano* pin-up, a muscle-bound fishmonger who had found a new vocation as he delighted tourists lifting a 22 kg *corvina*, or meagre, with the ease of a champion weightlifter. He seemed so taken with his celebrity status that, an hour later, despite a steady stream of visitors, flashes were still firing and he hadn't shifted as much as a sardine.

Less familiar to the visitor are the stalls of salted fish that are such a feature of the Spanish market. Salting was once a means of preserving cod for long sea voyages or for the Catholic consumer inland, who needed his Friday fish. Today salt cod, or *bacalao*, is hailed as the 'ham of the sea' and features on upmarket menus from the Basque coast to the inland plains of Castille. The cured anchovies of Cantabria and the Costa Brava are given cult status too, nibbled alongside a glass of local wine. Further south *mojama*, or salted tuna, and *botargo*, or the pressed grey mullet roe, are the stars of the show. Wafer-thin slices, along with a dash of extra virgin olive oil, make a simple and delicious starter.

suquet de peix
catalan fish hotpot

Here is one of the most celebrated dishes of the Costa Brava; a hotpot of the freshest fish cooked with the mixture of onions and tomatoes known as a *sofregit*. The *sofregit* is one of the keystones of Catalan cooking and the real secret to success is to fry the onions and tomatoes slowly until you have a rich, brick-coloured paste.

The stew is finished with a *picada*, another Catalan classic consisting of a ground mixture of herbs, garlic, nuts and bread that miraculously thickens, enriches and seasons the dish in one go.

serves 6

4 tbsp olive oil	canned tomatoes, drained
4 garlic cloves	450 g/1 lb waxy potatoes, peeled
1 slice of good white bread	and thinly sliced
2 tbsp plain flour	600–800 ml/1–1⅓ pints fish stock
salt and freshly ground black pepper	(see right)
1 kg/2¼ lb fresh white fish fillet,	1 bay leaf
such as monkfish, bream, sea	30 g/1 oz roasted almonds
bass, halibut, cod or hake,	2 fresh sprigs of parsley, finely
skinned and cut into large pieces	chopped
100 ml/3½ fl oz brandy	to serve
3 onions, diced	fresh bread
8 ripe tomatoes, grated or 400 g/14oz	*Allioli* (see page 114)

Begin by heating half the olive oil in a pan and frying the garlic cloves until they turn golden. Remove and set aside for the *picada*. Next add the slice of bread to the pan and fry until it is browned on both sides. Set aside with the garlic.

Mix the flour and ½ tsp salt together on a plate, dredge the fish steaks in the mixture, shaking off any excess flour, then fry the fish in the garlic oil. You may need to add a couple of tablespoons of extra oil to the pan. Once the fish is golden on both sides pour on the brandy and ignite or, if you are afraid of losing your eyebrows, cook over a high heat until the pan is almost dry. Remove the fish from the pan and set aside.

Now it is time to make the *sofregit*. In the same pan, adding a touch more oil if necessary, fry the onions until really soft and beginning to caramelize. Add the grated tomato flesh and continue to cook until you have a thick paste. Add the potatoes, fish stock and bay leaf and cook for about 15 minutes, or until the potatoes are tender. Season with salt and pepper to taste.

Meanwhile, make the *picada* by grinding together the reserved garlic and bread with the roasted almonds and parsley until you have a smooth paste. Energetic purists will stick to the traditional mortar and pestle for this, while I happily resort to the food processor!

Add the *picada* to the pan together with the fish and simmer for about 5 minutes until the fish is just cooked through, a little longer if you are using monkfish.

Serve with good bread and a generous dollop of *Allioli*.

Making a simple fish stock

Many seafood dishes are cooked with fish stock, the quality of which will determine the success of the final dish. It amazes me how many people will splash out on an expensive fish only to cook it with a stock cube.

Making tasty stock is very easy if you remember a few basic points. Do not use oily fish for stocks. Wash the fish bones and heads carefully to remove any blood that could taint the flavour of the stock. Add the bones, heads and skin to just enough cold water to cover, together with a halved onion, a chopped carrot and a stick of celery. You may like to add a bay leaf, parsley stalks and a few peppercorns too. Simmer for 20 minutes and strain, any longer and the stock may taste bitter. Do not let the stock boil.

It's hardly 'rocket science' and your friendly fishmonger will often be happy to part with a few extra bones for nothing.

dorada al horno
baked gilt-head bream

Shoals of exotic, glistening seafood piled on ice are a glorious sight, but when it comes to the crunch a huge array of unfamiliar fish can be a daunting prospect for any but the most experienced chef. It is all too easy to plump for the more familiar, bone-free, portion-sized piece of tuna or salmon. Yet roasting a whole fish in the oven is one of the simplest and tastiest things to do with a deliciously fresh fish.

On Spain's Mediterranean coast the *dorada*, or gilt-head bream, would be the top contender for such a treatment. With its painted golden brow and cheeks it is the king of the sea bream family, a title earned not just for its good looks, but for texture and flavour too. The *dorada*'s slightly less distinguished cousin the *pargo*, or common or red sea bream, would be equally fit for the job too.

Is it cooked?
When baking a whole fish the dorsal fin will pull away easily once the flesh is cooked. The flakes of the fish become more distinguishable once cooked. They will flake apart when you press the flesh and the shiny translucent flesh will have also become opaque.

serves 4

3 large potatoes, peeled and thinly sliced
4 tbsp olive oil
1 onion, sliced
2 x 675 g/1½ lb sea bream, scaled and gutted (cleaned)
salt and freshly ground black pepper

2 bay leaves
1 lemon, cut into wedges
1 small bunch of fresh parsley, chopped
3 garlic cloves, crushed
100 ml/3 fl oz wine

Preheat the oven to 200°C/400°F/Gas Mark 6.

Select a roasting tin large enough to hold your fish and arrange the potatoes over the base. Sprinkle over the olive oil and toss the potato slices around with your fingers ensuring that they are covered in the oil. Roast for 10 minutes. Do not be tempted to add any salt at this point; it will draw moisture out of the potatoes preventing them from browning.

Next add the onion and carefully stir into the potatoes turning them as you go. Return the tin to the oven and roast for a further 10 minutes until the potatoes and onions begin to gild.

Meanwhile, rinse the fish, removing any traces of blood, stubborn scales, fins and gills. It is an idea to leave the dorsal fin (the fin on its back) intact, to help check whether the fish is thoroughly cooked later on. Now make 2–3 diagonal slashes into the flesh on each side of the fish and season with salt and pepper.

Arrange the fish on top of the potatoes, inserting a bay leaf and a lemon wedge into each and squeezing the remaining lemon juice over the top of the fish. Sprinkle over the parsley, garlic and wine and roast for 15–20 minutes until the fish is cooked (see right). Serve at once.

Variations   You could stuff the fish with a *picadillo*, or finely chopped mixture, of fresh tomato, basil and green olives. I would love to serve this dish with some simply roasted red peppers (see page 144).

merluza en salsa verde
hake with parsley sauce

Hake, with its dense yet soft white flesh is possibly the country's favourite fish. Crate upon crate of these ugly, eel-like fish are landed every dawn on the wharf at Vigo's wholesale fish market. Much of the hake is caught by British boats but sold in Spain where it commands higher prices.

This is a classic recipe from the Northern Spanish kitchen. Each and every chef seems to have his own rendition of 'the' truly authentic recipe. Here you have it in its simplest form. However, you may like to add any of the following to the sauce: peas, asparagus tips, prawns, steamed clams, poached or boiled eggs.

serves 4

2 tbsp plain flour
salt
4 x 175–200 g/6–7 oz hake fillets
3 tbsp olive oil
2 garlic cloves, thinly sliced

4 tbsp dry white wine
2 tbsp water or fish stock
1 tbsp fresh parsley, finely chopped
Juice of ½ lemon (optional)

Mix the flour and a pinch of salt together on a plate, then dredge the fish steaks in the mixture, shaking off any excess flour.

Heat the olive oil in a large frying pan, add the garlic and fry until golden. Remove the garlic and set aside.

Add the fish skin-side up to the pan and fry for a few minutes, shaking the pan regularly. This not only ensures that the hake does not stick, it also helps to begin thickening the oil to a sauce-like consistency. Turn the fish over very carefully with a spatula or fish slice and continue to fry for a couple more minutes, shaking the pan as you go.

Add the wine together with the water or fish stock and simmer until the fish is just cooked through (see page 35). Add the reserved garlic and half of the parsley to the sauce. Taste to check the seasoning, adding salt or lemon juice if necessary.

Sprinkle the fish with the remaining parsley and serve right away with simple, boiled potatoes.

Buying fish
Fresh fish should be eaten as soon as possible after being caught. A strong 'fishy' aroma is a sure sign of stale fish; fresh fish should smell almost sweet.

The perfect fish should have bright, shining eyes and deep red gills, these go pale as the fish deteriorates. The flesh of fresh fish will feel firm to the touch and the skin will look glossy. Perhaps the best advice is to get to know your fishmonger and you will benefit from his expert knowledge.

Domestic refrigerators are not really cold enough to store fish for any length of time – if you are not using on the day of purchase, then store on ice on the bottom shelf. Fish does not freeze particularly well, it tends to dry out, unless you can buy it vacuum-packed.

Preparing fish
Recipes should be simple, with clean flavours that do not mask the subtle taste of the fish. Take care not to overcook fish, remember that it will continue to cook a little after it has been removed from the heat. Serve fish immediately after cooking.

atun adobado
marinated tuna

The warm waters around the Canary Islands are home to the *rabil*, or yellowfin tuna. This fish is prized for its firm, pale pink flesh, but can easily dry out during cooking if you're not careful. Hence this aromatic marinade which guarantees a gloriously juicy texture as well as a wonderful flavour. This recipe will also work well with any fresh tuna.

You will need to begin this dish 24 hours in advance.

serves 4

4 x 175–225 g/6–8 oz tuna steaks
2 tbsp olive oil
for the marinade
4 garlic cloves, crushed
1–2 chillies, according to your taste, very finely chopped
4 tbsp olive oil

1 tsp sweet non-smoked paprika
1 tsp dried oregano
½ tsp dried thyme
1 bay leaf
salt
4 tbsp white wine vinegar
4 tbsp white wine

Mix all the marinade ingredients together in a bowl.

Place the fish in a large non-reactive bowl or tray, pour over the marinade and turn the fish until coated. I sometimes use a zip-lock bag so that I can remove all the air and make sure the fish is completely covered in the marinade. Refrigerate for 24 hours.

Remove the fish from the refrigerator a few minutes before cooking, allowing it to reach room temperature.

Heat the olive oil in a frying pan over a high heat, add the tuna, reserving the marinade, and cook for a couple of minutes on each side, a little longer if you do not like eating rare fish.

Place the fish on a hot serving plate while you add the marinade to the pan. Leave this to bubble for a minute or two before pouring over the tuna. Serve at once.

Buying tips
The surface of the tuna flesh should never look dry or have a rainbow-like sheen. The belly, *ventresca*, is the most highly prized cut because of the high fat content. The flesh bastes itself as it cooks, remaining fabulously succulent. Tuna can range from deep, steak red to pale pink in colour depending on the species.

Know your tuna
Atún rojo, or bluefin tuna, is deep red in colour, has very dense firm flesh and a strong flavour. This is the most readily available tuna available in Spain.

Bonito is a smaller fish, not a true tuna, but similar in taste, popular in the North with dark flesh. It is quite similar to the bluefin and prepared in similar ways.

Albacora, *atún blanco*, *bonito del norte*, or albacore, is much paler in colour and more subtle in flavour. *Bonito del norte* is the king of all tuna as far as the Northern Spanish are concerned. You will find it canned too, at a price!

Rabil, or yellowfin tuna, has paler, pink flesh, a mild flavour and somewhat drier texture, so take care not to overcook it. This fish is popular eating in the Canary Islands.

Cooking tuna
Tuna has little fat and very meaty flesh. It is best cooked quickly to retain moisture – on the barbecue, under the grill or in the hot pan.

As rare as you dare is my advice, overcooked tuna has the texture of cardboard.

Remove the tuna from the refrigerator a few minutes before cooking, allowing it to reach room temperature. Otherwise your rare centre may remain unappetizingly cold.

sardinas rebozadas
sardine fritters

Stacks of wooden crates packed with glistening sardines hail the summertime in markets all around the Spanish coast. Sardines are astonishingly cheap compared with often prohibitively expensive white-fleshed fish such as sea bass or monkfish. Yet, there is no doubt that a stunningly fresh sardine, grilled directly over the barbecue coals, accompanied with nothing but rock salt and extra virgin olive oil, then gnawed somewhat unceremoniously in the fingers, is hard to beat. Equally delicious is this simple recipe gleaned from the fishermen in L'Ametlle del Mar, a busy port on the edge of the Ebro Delta.

Buying tips
Sardines should be exceptionally fresh so do look out for:
bright, glassy eyes;
scales that are shiny and completely intact; loose scales are a sign that the fish is past its best.

serves 4

8 x 110 g/4 oz sardines, scaled and filleted
1 tsp salt
1/2 tsp ground black pepper
1 tsp ground cumin
1 tbsp fresh parsley, very finely chopped

6 tbsp olive oil
2 eggs, beaten
100 g/4 oz plain flour
2 lemons, cut into wedges

Season the sardine fillets with the salt, pepper, cumin and parsley.

Next pour the olive oil into a large frying pan, to a depth of about 1 cm/1/2 inch and place over a high heat.

Meanwhile, set up your production line: a small bowl for the beaten eggs and a dinner plate for the flour. Dip the fish into the egg mixture, then turn in the flour.

Once the oil is really hot, begin to fry the fish fillets a few at a time until the batter becomes golden and the flesh is firm. This will take a matter of moments.

Drain the fish on kitchen paper and place in an oven to keep warm while you fry the remaining fillets.

Serve at once with wedges of lemon.

Tip   This would be delicious served as a starter with a fresh tomato sauce or make double quantities and serve as a light summer lunch with a green salad.

truchas al horno
baked trout

The town of Trevélez sits high in the Sierra Nevada. It is well known for its delicious trout, fished from the crystal clear waters of the river, but its true claim to fame is the curing of excellent quality *jamón Serrano*. The cool dry mountain air is ideal for the process and raw hams are brought here from all over Spain. The entire town is pervaded by the wafts of ham.

My visit was most untimely, five months pregnant and cured meat among the dreaded list of forbidden fruits; it was torture. Thankfully I could eat this dish since the ham is crisped in the oven. The combination of trout and *jamón* is a classic all over Spain. The saltiness of the ham cuts beautifully through the richness of the oily fish.

serves 4

4 tbsp olive oil
2 garlic cloves, finely diced
1 tbsp fresh parsley, finely chopped
1/2 tsp fresh rosemary, finely chopped
1/2 tsp fresh thyme, finely chopped

salt and freshly ground black pepper
4 x 225–350 g/8–12 oz brown or rainbow trout, scaled and gutted (cleaned)
8 thin slices of *jamón Serrano*

Preheat the oven to 200°C/400°F/Gas Mark 6.

Line a baking sheet or roasting tin with foil and oil with 1 tbsp olive oil.

Mix the garlic, herbs, a pinch of salt, pepper and 2 tbsp olive oil together in a bowl. Now spoon this aromatic paste into the body cavity of each fish.

Brush the outside of the trout with the remaining oil, then give each fish a waistcoat of ham, tucking the outside edges of the ham into the bellies. Bake in the oven for 15–20 minutes until the eyes are glazed, the flesh feels firm and the ham has crisped up. (See tips for baking whole fish, page 35.) Serve at once.

Tip Serve with *Patatas a lo Pobre* (see page 153) or, for a lighter touch, a green salad.

croquetas de bacalao
salt cod croquettes

Should cooking salt cod, or *bacalao*, seem a little daunting then here is a good place to start. A small amount of fish goes a long way and you will have a chance to experience how simple the soaking process is (see page 44).

Potato, rather than the more customary béchamel (see Partridge *Croquetas* on page 81), binds these melt-in-the-mouth salt cod croquettes giving them a wonderful texture. If the idea of deep-frying fills you with horror then you could shape these as flat discs and shallow-fry them instead, but then, of course, you will be making fishcakes and not *croquetas* at all. You will need to begin preparing your salt cod 24 hours in advance.

makes 12 croquetas

200 g/7 oz salt cod (dry weight), de-salted (see page 44)
1 bay leaf
2 large floury potatoes, about 300 g/ 11 oz, washed and unpeeled
2 tbsp fresh parsley, finely chopped
2 garlic cloves, crushed

salt and freshly ground black pepper
3 tbsp plain flour
vegetable oil, for frying

to serve
lemon wedges
mayonnaise (see page 114) or *Allioli* (see page 114)

Place the salt cod in a saucepan with the bay leaf and cover with cold water. Bring to the boil, then reduce the heat to a gentle simmer and cook for 3–4 minutes.

Remove the fish and place the potatoes in the same water, topping it up if necessary. Boil the potatoes until they are soft.

Meanwhile, skin and bone the fish, rubbing the flesh through your fingers ensuring that you have a completely bone-free purée. Here is a moment when you can use that miraculous piece of equipment, the *pasapurés* (see page 17).

Once the potatoes are cooked, drain and peel off the skins. Push the potatoes through a sieve or better still use the *pasapurés* again. This is not the time for lumpy mash.

Mix the fish, potato, parsley and garlic together in a bowl. Check the seasoning, it is unlikely that you will need any salt, but maybe a little black pepper would go down well.

Leave the mixture until cold, then, with wet hands, shape into small balls or cylinders. Put the flour on a large plate and roll the *croquetas* in the flour until coated. Set them aside until ready to cook. They can be made a day ahead of time, just cover well or your entire refrigerator will smell fishy.

When ready to cook, heat enough vegetable oil for frying in a deep pan (see tips on deep-frying page 81) until a bread cube sizzles and browns in 30 seconds. Deep-fry the *croquetas* in 2 batches until a deep golden brown colour.

Leave to drain on kitchen paper and serve immediately with lemon wedges and mayonnaise or *Allioli*.

43

ensalada de bacalao y naranja
salt cod, orange and black olive salad

Salt cod, or *bacalao*, is immensely popular in Spain, a hangover from the days before refrigeration when salting was one of the only means of preservation. Once soaked, the rather unappealing grey, pungent flesh is transformed beyond belief, so do not be put off.

Today *bacalao* graces the menus of top restaurants and commands ever increasing prices; a trend set to continue with diminishing cod stocks. And why bother eating cotton wool tomatoes and tasteless lettuces in mid-winter? Just a glance in the market will reveal that it is the time for oranges, curly endive and new season olives. This is a truly seasonal salad. You will need to begin preparing your salt cod 24 hours in advance.

Buying salt cod
The dry flesh should have a slightly grey rather than yellowish tone. 150–175g/5–6 oz dry salt cod will yield a good main course serving once soaked.

It is best to use loin, or *morro*, for main course dishes while the flatter, more economical belly, or *loncha*, is ideal for stripping into ribbons for salads.

Preparing salt cod
The cod should be soaked for anything between 24 and 48 hours depending on the size of the pieces, 24 hours will suffice for a thin piece of belly while 36 hours is usually about right for main course portions.

Place the cod in a large bowl of cold fresh water and refrigerate. You will need to change the water at 8–12 hourly intervals. It is an idea to taste the fish; a hint of saltiness is delicious.

serves 4

300 g/10 oz salt cod (dry weight), de-salted (see right)
3 large Valencia oranges
2 medium potatoes, peeled, boiled and left to go cold
2 handfuls of curly endive, washed and ripped into small pieces

½ sweet red onion, very finely sliced
12 black olives

for the dressing
4–5 tbsp extra virgin olive oil
salt and freshly ground black pepper

Remove the cod from the soaking water and dry off with kitchen paper. Next, rip the cod into thin strips, removing any bones or skin as you go.

Peel and slice the oranges into rounds, reserving any spare juice for the dressing. Slice the cold potatoes into small chunks or slices. Place all the salad ingredients together in a large bowl, reserving a few orange slices and olives for garnishing.

Now you can make the dressing, by mixing the reserved orange juice, the extra virgin olive oil and seasoning together in a bowl. This dressing is really a case of tasting as you go and the result should be quite sweet to counterbalance the salty cod.

Just prior to serving, toss the salad in the dressing and arrange the reserved orange slices and olives on top.

Variations   For a more exotic version, cherries can be substituted for the olives.

If salt cod is not your scene try this recipe replacing the fish with a large handful of roasted almonds and a couple of boiled eggs for a substantial vegetarian winter salad.

charcuterie

Mention the towns of Jabugo, Guijuelo or Montánchez and you are guaranteed to set a Spaniard's pulse racing, for these are the sacred cradles of the very best *Ibérico* ham and you will soon discover that *jamón* is virtually a religion here.

The *charcutería*, cured meat stall, is easy to spot with its cancan chorus line of ham legs dangling from huge hooks above the counter. Catching an assistant's eye can be quite a challenge amidst the forest of trotters. Black trotters, white trotters; it is all a matter of utmost importance to the ham lover. The *pata negra* belongs to the king of pigs, the hairy indigenous *Ibérico* race that produces the caviar of hams, while the paler is that of the European pink pig, an altogether different prospect in the world of *jamón* (see pages 48–9). Hand-cut slithers, or *virutas* of *Ibérico* ham are a just extravagance; the marbled flesh quite literally melts in your mouth. I once

watched an ancient Señora empty her purse to pay for four tiny slices. She placed the waxed paper package carefully in her handbag and set off home bearing her prize with a new sense of urgency. When it comes to *jamón*, nothing is wasted. Scraps from around the knuckle are chopped into small cubes and stirred into vegetable dishes, while ham bones give vital flavour to the *cocido*, or stew (see page 88), and dozens of other traditional stews.

Sometimes the chorus line is replaced with a firebrick red curtain of sausages, such is the case in Santiago de Compostela's market where the local, soft cooking *chorizo* takes precedent. It is the key ingredient in the traditional *Caldo Gallego*, a hearty soup with beans and potatoes. The *chorizo*'s distinctive colour and flavour is all down to paprika, *pimentón*, Spain's favourite spice. The *lacón*, a short-cured shoulder of ham is popular in Galicia too,

cooked with turnip tops. And, so it is that each region of the country has its own traditional speciality. The damp climate of Asturias made curing and air-drying nigh impossible so that the local *chorizo* and *morcilla*, or black pudding, have always been smoked to preserve them. Meanwhile, the dry mountain air of Andalucia's Sierra de Aracena proved perfect for curing hams.

It can all get quite confusing too. A *morcón* in Extremadura is a small rugby ball of pork, fat and paprika, a *chorizo* in disguise. Meanwhile, a few hundred kilometres to the east in Murcia, the spherical *morcón* is boiled rather than cured and sliced like a 'luncheon meat', a rather superior one of course. Salamanca is Iberian pig country and the locals take their *embutidos*, or cured meats, extremely seriously. Andres Vicente's stall in the municipal market is an unbelievable spectacle, with a vast array

of pork sausages, hams, shoulders, loins and tongues – smoked or plain, hard cured or soft. It would take days to taste your way through the selection, an ideal project for a short city break perhaps?

So, pork is without a doubt the star of the *charcutería* and, in fact, if you spot a *chacinería* that is all he will sell. However, there are a few other cured meats that deserve a mention:

In mountainous regions the white, paprika-free, *longanizas* or *salchichones* may be made with wild boar, or venison instead of, or in addition to, pork. León has its *cecina*, a cured beef, or less commonly horse, with a subtle smoked flavour that makes a wonderful starter with a dash of olive oil. A relative newcomer to the counter is the *jamón de pato*, or cured duck breast, produced in Navarra alongside *foie gras* and *confit*, French tastes that have recently taken Spain by storm.

plato de embutidos
cured meat platter

This is without a doubt the easiest, and yet arguably the most delicious starter in existence. A plate of carefully selected cured meat with a few tasty accompaniments, if you feel like it, although none are strictly necessary.

You could serve one or all of these cuts, the only rule being to allow about 80 g/3½ oz per person. As an absolute treat I would buy the more expensive *Ibérico* ham, or *Pata Negra* as it is known in Spain, but the more economical *Serrano* would be fabulous too. *Illustrated on page 51.*

serves 6

12 slices of *jamón* (see right)
12–18 slices of *salchichón*
  (see right)
12–18 slices of *lomo* (see right)

12–18 slices of cured *chorizo*
  (see right)
4 ripe figs, cut into quarters
2 tbsp caperberries

Arrange the meat, figs and caperberries attractively on a large platter and serve at room temperature.

Tip   Keeping blocks of each ingredient together will create more visual impact and certainly be easier to serve.

Cured pork

When buying any cured pork, whether it is ham, loin or sausage, you should be aware of two distinctly different products. Firstly there is the cured meat of the ordinary 'white' pig, usually referred to as *Serrano* that accounts for about 90% of the market, and secondly there is the highly exalted flesh of the native Iberian 'black', *Ibérico* or *Pata Negra*, pig that often commands truly exorbitant prices.

White pigs are given commercial feed and are usually intensively reared while most their hairy black cousins live a relatively charmed life under the cork oaks of the 'dehesa' in Western Spain. To confuse matters further there are three qualities of *Ibérico* pig: *pienso*, which is fed almost exclusively on grain, *recebo*, which is fattened up with grain on top of its free-range diet of acorns, and lastly, that caviar of the Spanish larder, the *bellota*, reared out in the oak forests snuffling up acorns, roots and herbs. *Ibérico* products have a refined, distinctly nutty flavour when compared with the more readily available *Serrano* meat.

Jamón is the cured leg of pork. The very best *Jamón Iberico de Bellota* is ideally carved off the bone by hand. It is usually served in wafer-thin *virutas*, or shavings, rather than large slices (see illustration on page 50) and the deep magenta flesh is marbled with delicious fat. White crystalline specks in the meat are good news too, the sure sign of an acorn-fed hog. This ham is best eaten alone with no accompaniments at all. The hams of Jabugo, Guijuelo and Montánchez are the most celebrated but by no means the only ones to look out for.

A good quality *Jamón Serrano* can be a real treat too: excellent in

(continues above right)

crema fría de melón con jamón
chilled melon soup with cured ham

Here is a modern day spin on the deservedly popular combination of melon and *jamón*, a fabulously refreshing starter for an oppressively hot day. You could stretch to some *virutas* of the very best *jamón Iberico* for this dish since you will not require a huge quantity. The *Piel de Sapo*, or 'toad skin', melon would be the gastronome's choice, but any ripe and tasty melon will do.

serves 4

1–2 ripe melons,
    about 1.5 kg/3 lb total
70 ml/2½ fl oz dry white wine to
    taste (optional)
2 tbsp caster sugar dissolved in
    4 tbsp water to taste (optional)

juice of ½ lemon to taste (optional)

to serve
ice cubes
freshly ground black pepper
100 g/4oz *jamón*, preferably
    ***Ibérico* (see opposite), shredded**

Halve the melon and scoop out the seeds into a sieve, then leave to drain over a bowl for about 10 minutes. We do not want to squander any juices. Remove the flesh from the skin. I find it easiest to slice the melon and cut off the flesh but you could scoop it out, if you prefer.

Next, purée the melon in a blender and taste. You may have selected the perfect melon and need no extra flavour at all. More likely you will need to add a little extra depth of flavour with the wine, more sweetness with the sugar or even a tart touch of lemon juice. Just play around until you are happy.

Transfer the soup to a container and leave to chill for at least an hour, making sure to cover the container otherwise the melon's seemingly innocuous scent will taint everything else in the refrigerator.

When ready to serve, pour the soup into chilled bowls, add an ice cube, a good sprinkling of black pepper and top with the *jamón*.

Tip   Is your melon is really ripe? Press on the stalk end and the melon should give a little. Sniff the bottom of the melon – a delicious sweet perfume is a sign of a melon in its prime. Do not delay in using because a ripe melon will deteriorate quickly.

a bread roll, with melon or figs and a wonderful base flavour for many cooked dishes. The *denominaciones* (see page 16) of Teruel and Trevélez produce some of the best.

Lomo embuchado or *Lomo curado* is the cured loin of pork. It resembles a thick sausage until you cut into it revealing the lean flesh. It is marinated with garlic and paprika, encased in a skin and then air-cured. *Lomo* is an expensive treat, usually eaten alone to appreciate its delicate flavour and very rarely used in cooking.

Chorizo is a sausage flavoured with paprika. There are dozens of varieties but a few main points to keep in mind. If you are planning on eating it raw you will need to buy a fully cured *chorizo*, such as the famous varieties from Navarra or Rioja. These are dense and firm and often sliced thinly like salami.

Meanwhile, the links of soft *chorizo* require cooking and may be hot, *picante*, or sweet, *dulce*. Dark horseshoes of knobbly *chorizo* from León are delicious sliced and cooked simply in wine or cider (see page 54). *Chorizo* is a key flavouring in many rice and pulse dishes. Two other famous sausages just about fit into this family too - the *Morcón*, from Extremadura and Andalucia, a miniature rugby ball of paprika spiced pork, and the *Sobrasada*, from Mallorca, which is a paprika and pork paste encased in a skin, and delicious spread on bread.

Salchichón is the Spanish salami. It is a mixture of pork and fat flavoured with pepper and other seasonings, such as garlic or herbs. Vic, in Catalonia is famed for its *salchichón* and also the long thin version called *fuet*, or whip.

champiñones con jamón y queso de cabra
mushrooms with ham and goat's cheese

Once bitten never forgotten. I ate these in a bar in Pamplona.

makes 6 *tapas* or 4 starter portions
4 tbsp olive oil
16–24 button or chestnut
 mushrooms, stalks removed
2 thick slices of *jamón Serrano*,
 chopped into small pieces
2 garlic cloves, crushed
150 g/5 oz goat's cheese,
 Montenebro would be my choice
2 tbsp fresh parsley, finely chopped
2 tbsp breadcrumbs

Preheat the grill to medium. Heat 3 tbsp olive oil in a frying pan, add the mushrooms, cut-side up, and fry over a high heat until they begin to colour (about 5 minutes). Remove and place in an ovenproof dish, cut-side up.

Next, in the same pan, fry the jamón until any fat begins to render. Add the garlic and stir until you smell wafts of garlic. Take off the heat.

Mix the jamón and garlic with the goat's cheese and most of the parsley until combined, then stuff the mushrooms with the mixture. Add the remaining olive oil to the breadcrumbs and sprinkle over the mushrooms.

Place under the medium-hot grill and cook until the cheese begins to melt and the breadcrumbs brown. Sprinkle with the remaining parsley and serve.

judías verdes con jamón
green beans with ham

I first savoured these beans at a small restaurant in Miranda del Castañar. The hilltop town is a medieval gem with narrow alleys, rambling stairways and old ladies huddled on street corners playing cards. We were occasionally jolted back into the 21st century by the roar of 'goooooooooool', the cry of an overexcited Spanish football commentator; it was the World Cup. It can be hard to sum up much of an appetite in the sweltering summer heat, but I'm always up for a plate of greens and, with the addition of the *jamón*, these are a most satisfying dish.

serves 4 as a starter
700 g/1½ lb flat green beans,
 trimmed
2 tbsp olive oil
2 thick slices of *jamón Serrano*,
 cut into small cubes including
 the fat
3 garlic cloves, finely sliced
1–2 tsp red wine vinegar
freshly ground black pepper or
 smoked paprika (optional)

First boil or steam the green beans until just tender and set aside.

Next heat the olive oil in a large frying pan, add the ham and fry until the fat begins to render. Add the garlic and continue to cook until it begins to turn golden.

Add the beans, stirring them to coat in the oil. Sprinkle with the vinegar and check the seasoning. The ham will probably provide enough salt but you may like to add a little pepper or paprika. Serve warm.

garbanzos con morcilla
chickpeas with black pudding

You are as likely to sit next to a Michelin-starred chef as a stallholder at the legendary Bar Pinotxo in Barcelona's Boqueria market. Brothers, Albert and Jordi, miraculously conjure up a stream of fabulous dishes right under your nose in their cupboard-sized kitchen. Meanwhile, their charismatic uncle, Juanito, charms and chats to the clients. It is a magic combination.

Chickpeas with black pudding may be served as a hearty breakfast for the hungry early risers – the market awakens at dawn – or as a lunchtime snack for businessmen or tourists.

serves 4–6

3 tbsp olive oil
2 onions, finely sliced
2 garlic cloves, crushed
1 tbsp chopped fresh parsley
2 tbsp sultanas
1 *morcilla* or black pudding, skin removed and chopped into small pieces

500 g/1 lb 2 oz cooked chickpeas, you will need to soak 250 g/9 oz if cooking from scratch
1 tbsp toasted pine kernels
a good pinch of rock salt

to serve
1 tbsp extra virgin olive oil
1 tbsp balsamic vinegar

Heat the olive oil in a frying pan, add the onions and fry over a low heat until soft and golden. Add the garlic, parsley and sultanas, then increase the heat and cook, stirring until the garlic just begins to colour.

Add the black pudding and continue to fry for a couple of minutes, crumbling up the meat with a wooden spoon as you go. Add the chickpeas and stir thoroughly to combine all the flavours.

Sprinkle over the pine kernels and rock salt and serve hot with a splash of extra virgin olive oil and some balsamic vinegar. Yes, I know it is Italian, but if Albert is happy to use it then so am I.

judiones con chorizo
chorizo with red pepper and butter beans

Here is a cheat's recipe; purists may balk at the idea of ready cooked beans, but this is one of those store-cupboard standby dishes that is fabulous to have up your sleeve. And, you could always cook the beans from scratch if you prefer.

The marriage of *chorizo* and pulses is just magical – they are combined in dozens of traditional slow-cooked dishes such as *Cocido* (see page 88) and *Fabada*. Here they are thrown together and cooked in a matter of moments with astonishingly good results.

serves 4–6

2 tbsp olive oil
2 onions, diced
1 red pepper, de-seeded and sliced
2 garlic cloves, diced
250 g/9 oz hot or sweet *chorizo*, sliced (see page 49)
2 x 400 g/14 oz cans *judiones* or butter beans
400 g/14 oz can chopped plum tomatoes
salt and freshly ground black pepper

to serve

1 tbsp fresh parsley, roughly chopped
drizzle of extra virgin olive oil

Heat the olive oil in a large pan, add the onions and red pepper and fry until they soften. Add the garlic and *chorizo* and cook until the *chorizo* fat has rendered down and the pan is swirling with its crimson juices.

Tip in the beans, stirring to cover them in the delicious oil. Add the tomatoes and cook for 10 minutes. Sprinkle with the parsley and the extra virgin olive oil before serving.

chorizo con vino o sidra
chorizo with wine or cider

No last minute shopping, a flash of the knife, a quick blitz in the oven and, hey presto, you have one of the tastiest nibbles imaginable.

Serves 4

300 g/10 oz hot or sweet *chorizo*, preferably the soft cooking variety, but cured will suffice (see page 49)
300 ml/10 fl oz dry cider or red wine
crusty country bread, to serve

Preheat the oven to 200°C/400°F/Gas Mark 6.

Slice the *chorizo* into 2.5 cm/1 inch discs and place in a small ovenproof dish, ideally a terracotta *cazuela*. Pour over the wine or cider and bake in the oven for 15–20 minutes until the surface of the alcohol is shimmering with the *chorizo* juices.

Serve while piping hot with good crusty bread.

meat

Many foreigners find the *carnicería* or butchers stall a rather disturbing sight, there is certainly no attempt to mask the origins of the miniature lamb cutlets or the petite veal tongues. There is no place for sentimentality when buying meat in the market. Entire carcasses are often butchered with remarkable dexterity right under the customer's nose. You could almost piece the animal back together like a jigsaw puzzle since most of the extremities and offal are on sale too. The range of meat on offer will depend on the region and also the size of the market.

Barcelona's Boquería is home to over 35 butchers. Many of them sell the celebrated veal from Gerona or lamb from the neighbouring region of Aragón, while others specialize in horse meat or kid. You can pick up beef from Galicia or even the Argentine; the Boquería is a truly cosmopolitan place. There are plenty of offal, *menudos* or *depojos*, stalls too.

Rugs of white tripe, glistening kidneys, livers and hearts all make delicious eating, given the right treatment. It has to be said that the cheaper offal recipes do usually require a lot more love and attention than a choice cut of meat. Nowadays the clientele tend to be older ladies with the time or inclination to invest in the preparation, or those who are watching their pennies. Traditional offal dishes such as the Catalan *Cap I Pota*, or stewed calf's head and foot, or the famed *Callos a la Madrileña*, Madrid-style tripe, are more likely to be found in the bar or local restaurant than in the home today.

Provincial markets still reflect the traditional livestock of the area although other meats are available too. Sheep have always been the top of the bill in the arid lands of Navarre, Aragón, Castille, Extremadura and Murcia where a cow wouldn't

stand a chance. In Aragón Zaragoza's municipal market is a lamb showcase, as well as the tiny milk-fed *corderos lechales* and the cuts of *ternasco*, or spring lamb (see page 62), there are sheep's heads, lengths of intestine wound up like balls of wool, pearly white feet and even bunches of tails for the strangely named dish of 'mountain asparagus'. Cattle are confined to the richer pasturelands of Northern Spain, but most are slaughtered young and consumed as veal, the precious grazing is required for the dairy herds. Galicia's veal, *ternera*, is reputedly the best in Spain while it is the Basque's who relish the huge rib steaks of the older ox, *buey*. Pork, however, can be found in every market in the land.

In the old days families used to raise their own pig, fed on the household leftovers. The *matanza*, or slaughter, was celebrated with a feast of fresh pork although most of the meat was transformed into *embutidos*, or cured meats to last the winter. The modern tendency towards apartment living has all but knocked the custom on the head. Nowadays pork is usually the most economical meat on the butcher's slab although there are a few dramatic exceptions. *Cochinillo*, or suckling pig is an expensive delicacy, ideally roasted in a wood-burning oven until it becomes so tender that it can reputedly be carved with a plate. Few would attempt to cook this at home but the upmarket *carnicería* often has a couple on display on the off chance. The fresh meat of the Iberian pig, best known for its celebrated cured ham is sometimes available too, at a price, but most is snapped up by restaurant chefs before the rest of us get a look in.

costillas con miel
honeyed spare ribs

Ribs are one of the most economical cuts of pork on offer. They are easy to prepare and fabulously sticky and satisfying to munch in the fingers. I came across 101 variations on this recipe: some used white wine or dry sherry instead of the lemon juice, others added a sprig of rosemary, a bay leaf, cloves or a chilli for extra flavour. So do feel free to improvise too.

I adore the simplicity and the sweet-sour nature of this version. You could finish cooking the ribs on the barbecue too if you enjoy your meat charred.

You will need to begin this recipe a few hours in advance.

serves 4.

1.5 kg/3 lb pork ribs
juice of 2 lemons
4 garlic cloves, crushed
a generous sprinkling of freshly
** ground black pepper**

3 tbsp runny honey
1 tbsp olive oil
½ tsp salt

Marinate the ribs with the lemon juice, garlic and pepper for at least a couple of hours in the refrigerator.

Preheat the oven to 180°C/350°F/Gas Mark 4.

Place the ribs in a roasting tin and cook for 1 hour until tender.

Remove the ribs from the oven. Increase the oven temperature to 220°C/425°F/Gas Mark 7.

Next, take 1 tbsp of the juices and mix with honey, olive oil and salt. Pour the honey mixture over the ribs and cook for about 20 minutes, basting a couple of times, until the juices begin to caramelize.

Serve at once.

Tip   A bitter salad of watercress or curly endive would make an ideal accompaniment, contrasting beautifully with the sweetness of the ribs.

Buying pork

In times gone by most families had their own pig, a kind of household waste disposal, which they fattened up during the year. The *matanza*, or slaughter was, and still is for some, a time for celebration, feasting and stocking the larder. Much of the meat was cured to last the winter while other cuts were eaten at once.

You may have qualms about tucking into the family pig, but at least it ensured a free-range animal reared on natural food, a far cry from much of the intensively farmed pork on offer in the shops today.

Do try to find a purveyor of *cerdo ecológico*, or organic pork, or that of a small-scale, specialist producer at least. Welfare concerns aside, the flavour and texture of the meat will be incomparable.

lomo adobado
marinated pork tenderloin

Marinated pork pops up all over Spain. It is a fiesta day classic in the Canary Islands, part of the *matanza* (see page 57) ritual in Galicia and a common bar snack in Andalucia where the pork is served on a small piece of bread and called a *montadito*. The meat is marinated for anything between 12 hours and 3 days and then fried on the *plancha*, or griddle, or roasted in the oven. The choice is yours.

You will need to begin this recipe at least a day in advance.

serves 4

2 x medium-sized pork tenderloins
1 tbsp olive oil
1 lemon, cut into wedges
for the marinade
6 garlic cloves
1/2 tsp salt
1 tbsp sweet paprika

1/2 tsp hot paprika
100 ml/3 1/2 fl oz white wine
2 tbsp wine vinegar
6 tbsp olive oil
2 tsp fresh or 1 tsp dried thyme
2 tsp fresh or 1 tsp dried oregano

Trim any excess fat or membrane from the pork.

Crush the garlic with the salt in a mortar with a pestle, then mix all the ingredients for the marinade together in a small dish, just big enough for the pork to fit snugly. Add the pork, turning to cover the meat in the marinade, cover and refrigerate overnight or keep for a few days, the flavours will only improve.

When you are ready to cook the pork, remove the tenderloin from the marinade and cut, slightly on the diagonal, into thin 1 cm/ 1/2 inch slices.

Heat a griddle or heavy frying pan with a little olive oil and fry the pork in batches. Do not be tempted to overcook the meat, it should still be a little pink and tender in the centre (see right).

Serve with the lemon wedges and a green salad or as montaditos on slices of bread topped with some grilled green peppers.

To roast the pork   Preheat the oven to 190°C/375°F/Gas Mark 5.

Sear the whole tenderloins on a very hot griddle or in a frying pan with a little olive oil. Once lightly browned return to the marinade and roast the pork for 20–30 minutes until just cooked through. The meat should remain a little pink in the centre.

Leave to rest for a few minutes while you boil down the marinade to a glossy sauce. Slice the pork thickly and serve as above.

Cooking pork

Many cuts of pork such as the loin or tenderloin are extremely lean and apt to dry out and turn leathery if you are not careful. Marinating, crumbing or wrapping in fat and bacon will help to protect the meat.

Pork is still often cooked to the point that it is devoid of any moisture at all. In the old days there was the fear of contracting trichinosis, whereas nowadays this risk is almost non-existent if buying pork from reliable sources. Use a meat thermometer if you feel cautious. The parasite would be killed in any case once the core temperature of your meat reaches 65°C/150°F, a far cry from the desiccated cardboard often served. In fact today the meat is served pink and juicy in many upbeat Spanish restaurants and delicious it is too.

libritos de cerdo
ham and cheese stuffed pork

Yet another example of the more positive face of ready-meals, these little 'books' of pork loin can often be purchased stuffed, crumbed and ready for the pan. If you are starting from scratch then slicing the pieces of pork open is your only challenge and I have found most butchers are very obliging and happy to cut the meat ready for stuffing. You could try using slices of aubergine instead of the pork for another simple supper dish.

serves 4

8 thick slices of pork loin
4 slices of cooked ham
4–8 slices of good melting cheese,
 such as young Mahón or
 Emmental

100 g/4 oz plain flour
2 eggs, beaten
150 g/5 oz breadcrumbs
4 tbsp olive oil

Cut the slices of pork loin horizontally until you can open them out like a book. You may be able to persuade your butcher to do this for you. Open out the pork slices and stuff them with a slice of ham and an equal-sized piece of cheese. Close the pork around the stuffing and press down firmly on a board.

Now for the production line: place the flour, beaten eggs and breadcrumbs on separate large plates. Dip the pork loin first in the flour, then the beaten egg and lastly in the breadcrumbs. Once all the pork is ready, and this can be prepared and refrigerated well ahead of time, it is time to heat the olive oil in a large frying pan.

Fry the pork, in batches, until crisp and golden. It will be just a matter of 2–3 minutes on each side.

Drain on kitchen paper and keep warm until all the meat is fried and ready to serve.

Tip Fabulous with a good tomato sauce or some gently fried piquillo peppers.

jarretes de cordero con aceitunas
spiced lamb shanks with olives

Even in Andalucia, after seven centuries of Moorish rule, North African inspired dishes such as this one are not as common as one might imagine. It can be a serious challenge tracking down coriander, a predominant flavour in Morocco, just a matter of miles away across the Straits of Gibraltar. So, I was thrilled to be arrested by its distinctive aroma under the Moorish archway of Málaga's bustling market. There were generous bunches of mint and parsley on offer too. Any of these herbs match well with the lamb, giving a burst of freshness to the slow-cooked spices. You will need to begin this recipe 24 hours in advance.

serves 4

4 lamb shanks
3 tbsp olive oil
3 onions, finely sliced
8 garlic cloves, unpeeled
1 tbsp plain flour
200 ml/7 fl oz white wine
200 ml/7 fl oz water
salt
200 g/7 oz stoned black olives

a handful of freshly chopped coriander, parsley or mint, to garnish

for the spice mix
1½ tsp freshly ground cinnamon
1½ tsp ground ginger
1 tsp freshly ground cumin
1 tsp freshly ground coriander
½ tsp hot non-smoked paprika

For the spice mix, mix all the ground spices together in a small bowl and rub them over the outside of the lamb shanks. Place the lamb in the refrigerator and leave to absorb the flavours overnight.

Preheat the oven to 170°C/325°F/Gas Mark 3.

Heat the olive oil in a terracotta *cazuela* or cast-iron casserole and brown the lamb shanks. Once the meat has seared, creating colour and flavour in your finished dish, you can set the shanks aside.

Next, using the same oil, fry the onions until they are soft and lightly browned. Add the garlic and flour and stir thoroughly until the flour begins to colour. Slowly add the wine, stirring all the time together with the water. Season with a little salt to taste.

Return the shanks to the casserole, cover with a tight-fitting lid and place in the oven. Traditionally the pot would remain on the stove, as few households had ovens in the old days. However, unless you are a pressure cooker enthusiast, I would recommend that you place the dish in the oven and go about your other business with no fear of a burnt bottom.

After 1½ hours, add the olives to the lamb and cook for a further 30 minutes, or until the meat is really tender.

Sprinkle with freshly chopped herbs and serve with chickpeas, couscous, mashed potato or a doorstep of good bread.

Buying lamb
Cordero lechal, milk-fed lamb, up to 1½ months old, is an extremely expensive delicacy that is best roasted in the domed, wood-fired ovens typical of Castilla and Aragón. The flesh is pale, incredibly tender and very delicately flavoured.
Ternasco, up to 4 months old, has just begun to feed on the fresh spring pastures. This is premium meat to serve simply roasted or grilled with no need for sauces, which may mask its subtle yet delicious flavour. Tiny grilled cutlets (about 6 per person) are fabulous served with a few roasted red peppers.
Cordero Pascual (Easter lamb), up to 1 year old, has deeper pink flesh, is not quite as tender as *ternasco* but has a wonderful depth of flavour. Leaner cuts are ideal for roasting and grilling whilst the neck, shoulder and shanks make fabulous stews and hotpots.
Carnero or *Oveja* (mutton), from animals of over 1 year old, is a bargain in Spain where younger, more delicate meat is preferred. Yet, the deep red flesh is ideal for some stews where long slow cooking will tenderize the tougher meat, and ingredients such as paprika and vinegar will counterbalance the stronger flavour.

pata de cordero con peras
braised leg of lamb with pears

It is no coincidence that this combination of meat and fruit may sound more like a recipe for a Moroccan tagine than a Spanish stew: it harks back to the time of the Moors. You could add some cumin, cinnamon and saffron for a more aromatic touch but this dish from Valencia really allows the flavour of the lamb to predominate. You will need to soak the beans overnight, although you could always cheat with ready-cooked beans from the market, or the can, for this recipe. Serving is easier if the leg has been boned and tied.

serves 4–6

250 g/9 oz *garrafó* or *judiones*, or large white haricot or butter beans, soaked overnight
1 bay leaf
1 tsp salt
1.5 kg /3¼ lb leg of lamb
salt and freshly ground black pepper
3 tbsp olive oil
3 medium onions, diced
4 garlic cloves, sliced

1 tsp sweet paprika
300 ml/10 fl oz beef, chicken or vegetable stock
2 small potatoes, cut into bite-sized dice
200 g/7 oz *ferraura* beans, or green/runner beans, trimmed and cut in half lengthways
4–6 small pears, Conference would be ideal, peeled, cored and halved

Drain the beans and place them in a pan of cold water with the bay leaf. Bring to the boil, skimming off any froth with a ladle then reduce the heat to a simmer and cook until almost tender, about an hour but maybe longer if the beans are older. Season with 1 tsp of salt.

Meanwhile, season the lamb with salt and pepper. Heat the olive oil in a large terracotta *cazuela* or cast-iron casserole and brown the lamb. Add the onions and cook until golden before adding the garlic and paprika. Once you can smell the garlic's wonderful aroma it is time to add the stock.

Cover the pan and simmer gently, turning the lamb over after about 30 minutes. Alternatively, you could place in an oven preheated to 170°C/325°F/Gas Mark 3.

After an hour add the potatoes to the lamb. To be truly authentic you should add the green beans at this stage too, but I prefer mine less cooked.

Once the potatoes are beginning to soften add the pears together with the drained beans and green beans, if you chose not to add them before, and cook for a further 20 minutes.

Carve the lamb and serve with the accompanying vegetables and pears.

riñones al jerez
kidneys with sherry

The stalls of offal or *menudencias/asaduras* are sometimes a rather disturbing sight for foreigners accustomed to a more sanitized approach to meat. Carefully arranged displays of heads, tongues, trotters and testicles may seem a little daunting, if not terrifying, to the novice chef, or spectator for that matter. The more familiar kidney seems a good place to start, especially since this classic recipe from Andalucia requires opening a bottle of sherry too; any excuse!

serves 4

675 g/1½lb lambs' or calves' kidneys prepared for cooking (see right) and cut into 2 cm/¾ inch thick slices
salt and freshly ground black pepper
2 tbsp olive oil
1 onion, finely diced

1 garlic clove, crushed
1 tbsp plain flour
100 ml/3½ fl oz beef stock, chicken stock or water
100 ml/3½ fl oz dry *Oloroso* sherry
1 bay leaf
1 tbsp chopped fresh parsley

Season the kidneys with ½ tsp salt and pepper. Heat the olive oil in a pan, add the kidneys and fry over a medium heat until just browned, overcooking is the kiss of death. Remove them to a warm plate.

Using the same oil, fry the onion until soft and golden. Add the garlic and fry until you smell its fabulous aroma. Next stir in the flour and cook for a minute or two. Pour over the stock or water, stirring all the time to avoid any lumps forming. Add the sherry and the bay leaf and simmer the sauce for 10 minutes.

Check the seasoning and add the kidneys to the sauce. Heat through gently for about 5 minutes. Feel free to investigate the kidney situation by cutting through a piece, it should still be a little pink.

Sprinkle with parsley and serve alone as a *tapas* treat or with plain, boiled rice as a more substantial supper dish.

Which type of kidney?
Calves, *ternera*, or lambs, *cordero*, kidneys are the mildest in flavour and the most tender, ideal for sautéing or grilling. Meanwhile, those of the pig, *cerdo*, or ox, *buey*, have a stronger taste and can be a little tough and so are more suited to slow cooked meaty stews.

Buying and preparing kidneys
Kidneys should be as fresh as possible, ideally removed from the fat, or suet, that surrounds them by the butcher as you buy them. They should look firm and shiny.

Cook the kidneys straight away as they can gain an unpleasant ammonia taste and smell if left to hang around.

Pig or ox kidney is often soaked for about 30 minutes in water with a tablespoon of vinegar or lemon juice to remove any ammonia flavour. However, very fresh lambs' or calves' kidneys do not require this treatment.

To prepare for cooking, peel the membrane off the outside of the kidney and remove as much of the fatty, white core as possible. Cut into thick slices or chunks depending on the dish.

Cooking kidneys
Kidney must be cooked quickly and served slightly pink or long and slow until tender. Anything in between and you are in for rubber bullets.

rabo de toro
braised oxtail

Rabo de toro is certainly the ultimate dish of the day during Sevilla's April *feria*, when the Real Maestranza bullring is packed with cigar-smoking spectators, pert-bottomed *matadors* and magnificent bulls. The *carne de lidia*, fighting bull meat, is available across the river at the nearby Mercado de Triana. The fastidious rearing and feeding of these powerful animals is a sure guarantee of fully flavoured meat. However, you may decide that the butcher's standard *rabo de buey*, or oxtail is a more readily available and less emotive choice. Whatever the case ask your butcher to chop up the oxtail unless you own a large cleaver or fancy a workout.

serves 4

3 tbsp plain flour	2 leeks, thoroughly washed
salt and freshly ground black	and sliced
pepper	4 garlic cloves, peeled but
2 kg/4½ lb oxtail, chopped	left whole
into pieces	2 bay leaves
3 tbsp olive oil	a small sprig of fresh thyme
3 onions, diced	3 cloves
3 carrots, sliced	1 bottle of red wine

Season the flour with salt and pepper, then dust the oxtail pieces with the mixture.

Heat the olive oil in a large cast-iron casserole and brown the oxtail a few at a time. Set aside as soon as they are browned. If the pan becomes dark and the oil is in any danger of burning deglaze the casserole (see below) between batches of meat.

Next, using the same oil, fry the onions, carrots, leeks and garlic over a low heat until soft and golden.

Add the bay leaves, thyme, cloves and wine and return the oxtail to the pan. Cover with a tight-fitting lid and simmer over an extremely low heat for about 3 hours, or until the meat is meltingly tender and falling off the bone. You may prefer to cook the oxtail in an oven preheated to 140°C/275°F/Gas Mark 1 and take the dog for a walk. Season before serving.

Tip Locals would eat this dish alone with bread but should you choose to serve it with mashed potatoes or rice it will easily stretch to feed six people.

Deglazing When searing meat for any stew or casserole you want to make the most of all the wonderful caramelized flavours on the bottom of the pan. The danger when dealing with multiple batches of meat is that the sediment and juices will burn before the browning job is done. So, between batches, just add a little wine or water to the pan and bring it up to the boil, loosening all the delicious bits. Reserve this liquid as stock for the dish, add a little more oil to the pan and continue to brown the meat.

Veal and beef in Spain

Ternera literally means veal, but this not the very young milk-fed variety, but pink meat from calves of anything up to ten months old. *Ternera* is immensely popular in Spain. The scarcer milk-fed veal or *ternera lechal* is available at a premium from the region of Ávila.

Carne de Añojo refers to the lean and tender meat or young beef, or yearling. Most beef, unless otherwise stated, will be in this category. The meat will be used for dishes such as *rosbif* or for simple steaks.

Carne de buey is less common and refers to meat from cattle of over two years of age, with deep red meat that requires plenty of hanging. Recipes such as the braised oxtail (see left) would ideally use this age of meat. The *carne de toro de lidia*, or fighting bull meat falls into this category too.

filetes de ternera   veal cutlets or escalopes

Lush grazing for cattle is extremely precious in Spain and, with the pasturelands of the north supporting mainly dairy herds, there is little space for maturing beef cattle. Most animals destined for the pot are slaughtered young and veal or *ternera* is always available in the market. Breaded or simply fried slices of veal are served in restaurants and households all over Spain.

filetes empanados
breaded veal escalopes

serves 4

4 x 150 g/5 oz veal chops or escalopes
juice of ½ lemon
salt and freshly ground black pepper
1 egg, beaten with 1 tbsp water
5 tbsp fresh breadcrumbs
1 tbsp chopped fresh parsley
3–4 tbsp olive oil
½ lemon, cut into wedges

Begin by flattening the slices of veal with a wooden mallet or rolling pin, be gentle or you will end up with something resembling steak tartar. Season the meat with the lemon juice, salt and pepper.

Now set up your production line: place the egg in a shallow dish, mix the breadcrumbs and parsley together and spread the mixture out on a large plate. First dip the veal in the egg and then turn in the breadcrumb mixture to coat thoroughly. The veal is now ready to go. If you want to get ahead of yourself you can prepare the meat to this point a few hours in advance.

Heat the olive oil in a large shallow frying pan and fry the veal gently until golden. If the oil is too hot you will burn the crust before the meat has cooked at all.

Serve at once with wedges of lemon. The meat is usually served alone or with a few chips, but you could accompany it with a simple tomato and garlic salad (see page 148).

filetes de ternera encebollados
veal escalopes with sweet onion sauce

serves 4

4 x 150 g/5 oz thinly sliced veal chops or escalopes
salt and freshly ground black pepper
2 tbsp olive oil

for the sauce
3 tbsp olive oil
2 onions, finely sliced
2 garlic cloves, crushed
50 ml/2 fl oz beef stock
50 ml/2 fl oz white wine

Begin by making the sauce. Heat the olive oil in a pan, add the onions and fry gently until soft and golden, at least 30 minutes. Add the garlic and stir until you smell its unmistakable aroma.

Pour over the stock and wine and boil until the liquid has reduced to a couple of tablespoons. Season with salt and pepper to taste. The sauce may be prepared ahead of time, if you prefer.

Meanwhile, you can prepare the veal. Flatten the meat carefully with a mallet or rolling pin, taking care not to tear the flesh and season with salt and pepper.

Heat the olive oil in a large shallow pan, add the meat and fry quickly. You may have to do this in 2 batches so have a warm plate at the ready.

Serve the veal with the sweet onions and some good bread or perhaps a spoonful of mashed potato to soak up the juices.

albóndigas
meatballs

Here is an absolute Spanish staple. Many market stalls sell *albóndigas* ready-made, to cook at home. They may be made with beef, pork or lamb, but most commonly with a blend of beef and pork. Once cooked they can sit in a tomato sauce and be reheated when you are ready.

serves 4

250 g/9 oz lean minced beef
250 g/9 oz lean minced pork
salt
a good grind of black pepper
a good pinch of freshly ground
nutmeg
2 garlic cloves, crushed
4 tbsp dry sherry
1 tbsp finely chopped fresh parsley
1 handful of breadcrumbs
2 eggs, separated
4 tbsp olive oil, for frying

100 g/4 oz plain white flour, for
dredging
for the sauce
1 onion, finely diced
2 garlic cloves, crushed
400 g/14 oz can chopped tomatoes
200 ml/7 fl oz meat or vegetable
stock
1 bay leaf
1 tsp of sweet or hot non-smoked
paprika
honey (optional)

Variations

You could make the meatballs using minced lamb, with cinnamon and a good pinch of dried cumin instead of the nutmeg. Substitute the sherry with lemon juice.

The tomato sauce could be zipped up too with a generous handful of freshly chopped mint or coriander and a good sprinkling of hot paprika. Serve this version with wedges of fresh lemon.

Place the minced meat in a large bowl with 1 tsp salt, the pepper, nutmeg, garlic, sherry, parsley and breadcrumbs and set aside for a couple of hours, if you have time, to let the flavours to develop.

Add the egg yolks to the meat and mix everything together, I like to use my fingers, ensuring that everything is well blended. In a separate clean bowl, whisk the egg whites until light and fluffy.

Roll a small ball of the mixture and fry in a little olive oil until brown. Taste and adjust the seasoning until you are happy.

Next shape the rest of the meat into walnut-sized balls. Tip your flour onto a wide tray and roll the meatballs first in the flour before dipping them in the egg white.

Heat the olive oil in a large pan and fry the meatballs in batches over a medium heat, shaking the pan from time to time to roll them over. As soon as they are browned and appetizing (they will continue to cook later) remove them from the pan and set aside.

Now it's time to make the sauce. Check the pan, if the oil looks too dark and burnt begin again, but ideally use the same pan with all its delicious meat juices to fry the onions until soft and translucent, then add the garlic and cook until just golden.

Add the tomatoes, stock and bay leaf and cook until the sauce is thoroughly combined and reduced a little. Season with the paprika and salt to taste. You may like to add a spoonful of honey if the sauce is acidic rather than sweet.

Add the meatballs to the sauce and cook until just firm.

macarrones
macaroni bake

We are talking simple home cooking here. One of those dishes that friends serve up for supper once they know you well and have no need to impress. It is delicious none the less.

serves 4

500 g/1 lb 2oz short Italian pasta, usually *penne*
1 bay leaf
1 tsp salt
3 tbsp olive oil
2 onions, diced
1 green pepper, diced
3 garlic cloves, crushed
150 g/5 oz minced beef
150 g/5 oz minced pork

50 g/2 oz pork liver pâté (optional)
300 ml/10 fl oz *tomate frito*, a sieved, fried tomato paste available in Spain or 400 g/14 oz can chopped tomatoes
salt and freshly ground black pepper
sugar to taste (optional)
100 g/4 oz grated cheese, such as Mahón
a little bit of butter

Preheat the oven to 180°C/350°F/Gas Mark 4.

Boil the pasta in plenty of water with the bay leaf and salt until just cooked (*al dente*). Drain the pasta and stir in 1 tbsp olive oil to prevent it sticking together.

Next heat the remaining olive oil in a pan, add the onions and green pepper and fry until they soften. Add the garlic and cook until pale golden. Add the minced meat breaking it up with a wooden spoon as you go.

Once the meat has browned slightly add the pâté, if using, and stir over the heat for a couple of minutes. Pour in the tomato and simmer over a medium heat for 10 minutes until the sauce has thickened. Taste and adjust the seasoning with salt, pepper and even a little sugar to counterbalance the acidity of the tomatoes if necessary.

Stir the meat sauce into the pasta and place in an ovenproof dish. Sprinkle with grated cheese and a few slithers of butter and bake in the oven for 20 minutes.

Tips   You may like to zap the dish under the grill for a moment or two for a really deliciously browned cheese topping.

The dish can be completely assembled ahead of time and then baked just before serving. Remember to add an extra 5–10 minutes to the cooking time if it is coming straight from a cold refrigerator.

Variations   The pork liver pâté is a trick of Isabel Jiménez's, the Cirera family's cook, and it certainly seems to give these *Macarrones* the edge. However, do feel free to leave it out if you are throwing the dish together and have none to hand.

Mushrooms could be added to the dish. Add them to the pan after the meat.

Pasta
Pasta dishes are popular in Spain particularly Catalonia, a region that absorbed a great wave of Italian immigrants in the 19th century. *Canalones*, Canneloni, have become a classic dish of the Catalan kitchen served in many a respected restaurant, while the less exalted plate of *macarrones* is more likely to make its way onto the *menú del dia*, or set menu at the local bar.

poultry and game

The town of Vilafranca de Penedés in Catalonia is well known for its poultry. Every Saturday smallholders and collectors come to peruse the baskets and cages of live fowl on offer. Chickens are snapped up for breeding and egg laying while some of the more exotic cockerels and duck will strut their stuff as showpieces in the enthusiasts' back yards. The pinnacle of the calendar comes in December at the Fira del Gall, or Cockerel Fair when discerning cooks come from afar to purchase their Christmas bird. It's an annual tradition, greeted with enthusiasm by the entire family. More importantly it is a way of guaranteeing the provenance of the festive feast.

Proud farmers and breeders give first hand information about their poultry before any money changes hands. Then it is up to the customer to carry his bird to a large temporary shed where children witness cockerels, capons, hens or ducks being handed over the

counter to meet their death, but there is no bloodthirsty rubbernecking. Families can go about the rest of the shopping, have a leisurely cup of coffee and return to collect their oven-ready bird a couple of hours later.

However, much poultry, chicken in particular, has suffered the same hideous fate in Spain as elsewhere in the western world. Tasteless factory-farmed flesh from luckless fowl packed into huge barns has sullied its good name. Many consumers have been lured into seizing a bargain at the expense of flavour, and animal welfare. It seems bizarre to consider that chicken was once the *fiesta* day treat, and even more unthinkable that, in Northern Catalonia, the dish was padded out with more readily available lobster and prawns to feed the crowds. Yet taste a true, free-range, farm-reared chicken and the notion no longer seems strange.

Many market stalls sell *pollo de granja* or *pollo de corral*, free-range chicken, alongside farmed rabbit.

There are countless wonderfully simple and tasty recipes for both but few make it outside of the home kitchen. The truth is that most restaurants consider such dishes far too commonplace. There is the *gallina*, or boiling fowl too, a particularly flavoursome choice when it comes to stocks and *cocidos*, or stews. Meanwhile, farmed quail and squab are given a more elevated status, often cooked with fruit sauces that hark back to the time of the Moors. Duck and goose are favourites in the Northeast combined with turnips, pears, figs or prunes. French influence is strong too with *confit* and *foie gras* appearing on upmarket menus with increasing regularity. Turkey is a Christmas treat for some, stuffed with apricots, chestnuts, sausage and herbs but is also available all year round.

In autumn the shooting season begins in earnest making the countryside a hazardous place to wander. Feathered game often adorns the poultry stall, although hanging times vary with the weather, and much is plucked and drawn within a day of being shot. The red-legged partridge is without a doubt the most plentiful game bird on offer, particularly in Castille. But wild duck, quail, wood pigeon and pheasant are sometimes available. Many game birds are pickled in escabeche, a wine and vinegar marinade that has a dual purpose, simultaneously moistening and preserving the lean flesh.

Much of the Spanish landscape is rugged and mountainous, making a great habitat for rabbit, hare, deer, wild boar and even the odd bear. Wild rabbit is a common sight in many markets while specialist stalls deal with the larger game. Rich game stews made with hare, venison or boar are often flavoured with wine, herbs and chocolate, while the bear stew once popular in Asturias has thankfully been relegated to the history books.

pollastre a la catalana
catalan chicken

Fruit is often used in savoury dishes, a hint of Spain's Moorish heritage. Don't be tempted to cut down on the generous quantities of apricots, sultanas and nuts in the recipe, they contrast beautifully with the salty bacon. You will need to begin this dish a couple of hours in advance.

serves 4

100 g/4 oz dried apricots
100 g/4 oz sultanas
70 ml/2½ fl oz brandy
1 chicken, cut into 8 portions, or 4 chicken legs, jointed
1 tsp salt
3 tbsp olive oil
200 g/7 oz unsmoked bacon, cut into small pieces
3 Spanish onions, diced
1 head of garlic, cloves peeled but left whole

2 large, ripe tomatoes, grated (see page 152)
a small bunch of fresh thyme, rosemary, parsley and a bay leaf tied with string
60 g/2½oz toasted pine kernels
100 ml/3½fl oz dry white wine
600–750 ml/1–1¼ pints chicken stock (see right)
crusty bread, to serve (optional)

Begin by soaking the dried fruit in a small bowl with the brandy. Leave to macerate for a couple of hours.

Season the chicken pieces with a little salt. Heat the olive oil in a large frying pan, add the chicken and brown over a high heat until crisp and golden, then set aside.

Pour the oil from the frying pan into a terracotta *cazuela* or cast-iron casserole. Add the bacon and fry over a medium heat until it begins to brown.

Next add the onions, the garlic cloves, the tomato flesh and the herbs. Give everything a good stir before adding the chicken pieces. Keep the pan bubbling over a medium heat until the onion and garlic colour, but do not let them burn.

Add the soaked dried fruit, pine kernels, wine and half the stock to the chicken and continue to simmer over a medium heat until the flesh is cooked through and the juices run clear, about 20–30 minutes depending on the size of the portions or joints. Add more stock if necessary, as the liquid reduces. You should have plenty of sauce so make sure you have some good bread to mop up the juices.

Tip   You may like to cook the chicken in the oven, giving a crisper skin. Preheat the oven to 190°C/375°F/Gas Mark 5 and cook for about 30–40 minutes, or until the juices run clear.

Making stock
Place the chicken bones in a large saucepan and add enough water to cover. You can also use chicken wings, which are a bargain if you have no leftover carcass. You may like to add any or all of the following to the bones: carrot, leek, onion, parsley stalks, a stick of celery, or a few peppercorns. However, the bones alone will produce a good base. The only hard and fast rule – never add salt.

Bring the water to the boil and remove the frothy scum from the top. Next reduce the heat and simmer gently for 2–3 hours.

Strain the stock and remove the fat, leave to cool slightly and then skim it off with a spoon or mop it up by laying kitchen paper over the liquid for a second. Reduce the liquid until well flavoured and then refrigerate for 2–3 days or freeze and use as required.

pechuga rellena con pisto
stuffed chicken breast with pisto

Stuffed chicken breasts are commonly available at the market stall, a type of 'ready meal' to throw in the pan or the oven when you get home. This combination takes little time to prepare yourself and is always a winner with children.

I like to bake the chicken breasts in the oven with the *pisto* to keep the meat moist, but you may prefer to simply fry them in the pan a little longer until thoroughly cooked through and then serve with wedges of lemon.

serves 4

4 medium chicken breasts
4 slices of ham such as *jamón York*, cooked ham rather than cured
4 slices of mild cow's milk cheese such as young Mahón, or the less authentic Emmental

3 tbsp plain flour
4 tsp salt and a little freshly ground black pepper
2 tbsp olive oil
1 x *Pisto* recipe (see page 152)

Preheat the oven to 180°C/350°F/Gas Mark 4.

Cut each chicken breast horizontally and open it up like a book. Lay the 4 breasts on a board and cover with a sheet of clingfilm or greaseproof paper. Next, using a rolling pin, beat out the meat carefully until it is all roughly the same thickness. Place a slice of ham and a slice of cheese onto each breast and fold the chicken back over to close.

Place the flour on a large plate and season with the salt and pepper, then dip each breast in the mixture to coat.

Heat the olive oil in a large frying pan, add the chicken and fry until golden on both sides. Next place the chicken in a small terracotta *cazuela* or ovenproof dish. Spoon over the *pisto* and bake in the oven for about 20 minutes, or until the chicken feels firm and thoroughly cooked through.

Buying chicken
Always buy the best chicken you can afford – intensively farmed chicken is tasteless, never mind the welfare considerations. Free range, *pollo de granja* or *pollo de corral* or, better still, organic, *ecológico*, is the way to go.

Buying a whole bird will give you much better value as you can use the bones for invaluable stock. If you don't get around to making it straight away you could freeze the carcass and have a stock 'fest' once you have amassed a few birds.

pollo con aceitunas
chicken with olives

You seldom find chicken served in a restaurant unless you plump for the bargain three-course *menú del dia*, or menu of the day. Chicken is considered homely, comfort food. Simple roast chicken can often be snapped up from the market van, cooked on a spit and flavoured with a few fresh herbs. The smell of crisping skin wafts around the stalls, making it nigh impossible to concentrate on the rest of the shopping. Chicken also finds its way into numerous regional dishes such as this one from Andalucia with its signature hint of sherry.

Cooking chicken
Chicken breasts always cook more quickly than legs so, when cooking casseroles, it is a good idea to remove the breasts about two-thirds of the way through the cooking time. Place them back in the pan for the last few minutes to warm through thoroughly. I like to leave chicken with the skin on, because it keeps the meat moist during cooking. You can always remove the skin, if you prefer, before serving.

serves 4

1.8 kg/4 lb chicken, jointed into 4 pieces, or 4 chicken legs
salt
3 tbsp olive oil
1/2 tbsp fresh rosemary, finely chopped
1/2 tbsp fresh thyme, leaves removed from stems
10 fresh mint leaves, finely chopped
1 tsp sweet paprika
2 onions, cut into fine slices
6 garlic cloves, left whole
1 small dried chilli
70 ml/2 1/2 fl oz dry sherry
150 g/6 oz black olives
1 lemon, quartered

Preheat the oven to 190°C/375°F/Gas Mark 5.

Season the chicken with salt. Heat the olive oil in a pan, a terracotta *cazuela* is ideal for cooking this dish, but any large, low-sided pan will do. Add the chicken pieces and fry until the skin crisps and turns golden.

Remove the chicken from the pan, place in a bowl and toss with the fresh herbs and paprika.

Return the pan to the heat and, using the same oil, fry the onions until they begin to brown. Add the garlic and chilli and continue to cook until the garlic begins to colour too. Take great care not to burn the garlic: burnt garlic tastes bitter and can ruin an entire dish.

Add the chicken to the pan together with any loose herbs from the bowl. Pour in the sherry and bake in the oven for about 40 minutes until the chicken is almost ready.

Add the black olives with the lemon quarters and return the chicken to the oven for about 5 minutes. Ensure that the chicken is thoroughly cooked before serving.

Variation   This dish is usually served with plenty of white bread, but you could choose to accompany it with rice or mashed potato to soak up some of the delicious juices.

higaditos salteados
sautéed chicken livers

The delectable taste of chicken liver somehow belies its economical origins. Here is a quick, delicious snack or a wonderful starter. It is worth keeping some livers in the freezer for this dish alone.

Grapes make a great accompaniment to the livers. They are traditionally served peeled, so I am told. Quite frankly life's too short. In any case, have you ever been bothered by a grape skin? Ironically I have, but only when trying to guzzle my obligatory dozen grapes, in time with the chimes of the New Year's Eve bells, as is the custom in Spain. Then the tiny cans of ready-peeled and counted grapes can prove quite an advantage.

Buying and preparing chicken livers

Avoid factory-farmed chicken livers if you can; a free-range chicken such as a *pollo de granja* or *pollo de corral* will have a better liver as well as meat. Trim away any green-tinged liver, it is not off, but indicates contact with the bile and its bitterness can taint a dish. Also remove any of the white connecting threads.

serves 4

3 tbsp olive oil
1 onion, finely sliced
100 g/4 oz *panceta* or bacon, finely diced
500 g/1 lb 2 oz chicken livers, cleaned and prepared (see right)
100 ml/3½ fl oz dry *fino* sherry
1 tsp fresh thyme leaves

1 tbsp fresh parsley, freshly chopped
salt and freshly ground black pepper

to serve

small bunch of seedless grapes
fried bread or crisp white toast

Heat 2 tbsp of the olive oil in a frying pan, add the onion and fry gently for about 30 minutes until they are really soft and golden.

Meanwhile, fry the *panceta* or bacon in the remaining oil until any fat has rendered down.

When almost ready to serve, add the livers to the bacon and brown over a high heat. Add the onion together with the sherry, thyme, half of the parsley and a touch of salt and pepper and cook for about 5 minutes. Check and adjust the seasoning if necessary.

Serve with the remaining parsley, grapes and toast or fried bread.

perdiz en escabeche
pickled partridge

An *escabeche* is an ancient means of preserving poultry or fish in a highly acidic mixture of wine and vinegar. The dish not only keeps for a few days but improves with time too, making it an ideal do-ahead dish for entertaining.

Game birds are lean and do have a tendency to dry out during cooking if you are not careful. Sitting in this piquant marinade will ensure that the flesh becomes tender and juicy. Quail, chicken, pheasant and even rabbit are also fabulous prepared in this way (see cooking times right). You will need to prepare this dish at least 24 hours in advance.

Using the recipe for other *escabeches*
Quail: simmer for 25 minutes.
Chicken quarters: simmer for 45 minutes to an hour. Ensure that the chicken is thoroughly cooked through before leaving to marinate.
Rabbit quarters: simmer for 45 minutes to an hour, or until tender.

serves 4

2 partridge, or 4 if you have large appetites, split in half
salt and freshly ground black pepper
2 tbsp olive oil
1 onion, finely chopped
2 carrots, finely sliced
3 garlic cloves, peeled but left whole
300 ml/10 fl oz white wine
300 ml/10 fl oz wine vinegar

300 ml/10 fl oz water or chicken stock
12 black peppercorns
pinch of saffron strands
3 bay leaves
1 sprig of fresh thyme
1 tsp hot or sweet paprika

to serve
1 lemon, sliced
a handful of fresh parsley, chopped
extra virgin olive oil

Begin by seasoning the partridge halves with salt and pepper.

Heat the olive oil in a large frying pan, add the partridge halves and fry until they begin to brown. Remove the partridges with a slotted spoon and add the onion and carrots to the pan. Fry for 10 minutes, then add the garlic and cook gently until it has turned pale gold. Take care not to burn the garlic.

Pour in the wine, vinegar and water or stock together with the peppercorns, saffron, bay leaves, thyme, paprika and a good pinch of salt. Bring everything to the boil then pop in the partridge. Reduce the heat and simmer, covered, for 30 minutes.

Transfer the partridge and vegetables to a small dish and pour over the liquid. Now the important bit: the marinade must completely cover the partridge if it is to act as a preservative. Leave to cool and then refrigerate for at least 24 hours, or better still a couple of days.

Serve the partridge and vegetables with a little juice, lemon slices, chopped parsley and a dash of really good extra virgin olive oil. The dish is usually served alone, but I love to have a crisp green salad alongside.

croquetas de perdiz y jamón
partridge and ham croquettes

The red-legged partridge is a popular and plentiful game bird in much of Spain. During the shooting season from October to March you will have no problem procuring one from the local market, feathers on or plucked and ready to go. In summertime you may like to try this recipe with chicken instead.

makes 12 croquettes

3 tbsp olive oil
1 partridge
1 onion, quartered
1 bay leaf
300 ml/10 fl oz water
1/2 small onion, very finely diced
4 tbsp plain flour
250 ml/8 fl oz mixture of milk and stock from the partridge

2 thick slices of *jamón Serrano*, about 75 g/3 oz
salt and freshly ground black pepper
freshly grated nutmeg
200 g/7 oz fine white, dried breadcrumbs
2 medium eggs, beaten with a little water
mild olive or vegetable oil, for frying

Heat 1 tbsp olive oil in a small pan or casserole, add the partridge and brown for a few minutes. Add the onion quarters, bay leaf and water, then cover and simmer until the partridge is cooked, about 20–30 minutes depending on the size of the bird.

Leave the bird to cool slightly before removing all the meat from the carcass and chopping or mincing it very finely indeed. Strain the cooking stock and reserve.

Heat the remaining olive oil in a saucepan, add the finely diced onion and fry until soft. Sprinkle over the flour and cook for a couple of minutes. Slowly add the milk and stock, stirring as if you were making a béchamel sauce. Boil the mixture for 2 minutes until it becomes really thick and shiny.

Next add the partridge and the *jamón*. Season with salt, pepper and nutmeg to taste. Take care as the *jamón* could be quite salty already. Spread the mixture in a thick layer on a flat dish and leave to cool. Chill for at least 2 hours, preferably overnight, until firm enough to handle.

Now for the production line: place half the breadcrumbs (once these are used up start again with the other half, as they can become quite lumpy) and beaten eggs in 2 wide dishes alongside a tray ready for the croquettes.

Using a knife, mark the chilled mixture into 12 bricks. Using your hands, roll each brick into a ball or cylinder. A bowl of warm water is ideal for keeping your hands damp and preventing them becoming too sticky. Dip in the breadcrumbs, then the egg and then back in the crumbs. Chill the croquettes for at least 1 hour, or freeze until ready to use.

Heat enough oil for frying in a deep-fat fryer or deep frying pan until a cube of bread browns in 30 seconds. You will need to submerge the croquettes so make sure there is enough oil in the pan. Fry them (see right) until golden brown, then drain on kitchen paper and serve at once.

Frying tips
A deep-fat fryer is the safest and most efficient way of frying, set at a medium heat of 190°C/375°F for *croquetas*. If you are using a pan, make sure you only half-fill it, as the oil will expand upon heating. Take care to heat the fat to the right temperature, a cube of bread should sizzle and brown in 30 seconds; any slower and the food will become fatty and soggy, any faster and you will not cook the centre properly or the *croquetas* may burst.

Always fry food in small batches; too much in one go will drastically lower the temperature of the oil.

Strain the cooled oil after use and discard as soon as it becomes dark or cloudy.

anec rostit amb prunes i pinyons
roast duck with prunes and pine kernels

Every year, on the last weekend before Christmas, the town of Vilafranca de Penedès in Catalonia hosts a huge poultry market: the *Fira del Gall*, or Cockerel Fair. The region is famed for its delicious free-range poultry. Families crowd into the Ramblas, the tree lined promenade, to select their Christmas dinner. Prize birds strut their stuff in large cages and corrals: cockerels, capons, hens, geese, turkey and duck. Toddlers pose for the annual festive photograph while cooks deliberate over which bird will grace their table.

I was struck by the show of tearful tenderness as a small boy patted a duck farewell before it was handed over to be prepared for the pot. This is stark reality – return in an hour and the bird is plucked and drawn.

Here is a much-celebrated local recipe for duck, but there are countless variations so do feel free to improvise too.

serves 4

1.5–2 kg/3¼ –4½ lb duck
salt and freshly ground black
  pepper
1 bay leaf
1 fresh sprig of thyme
½ stick cinnamon
1 onion, quartered
1 carrot, peeled but left whole
1 ripe tomato, left whole

1 tbsp olive oil
150 ml/5 fl oz *Vi Ranci* or *Oloroso*
  sherry (see page 16)
150 ml/5 fl oz water
12 ready-to-eat prunes, or dried
  prunes soaked for at least an
  hour in hot water
50 g/2 oz pine kernels, toasted
  (see page 108)

Preheat the oven to 200°C/400°F/Gas Mark 6.

Prick the duck all over with a fork and season with salt and pepper.

Place the bay leaf, thyme and cinnamon inside the duck and place the vegetables into a large roasting tin with the olive oil. Put the duck on a rack in the roasting tin above the vegetables.

Roast the duck breast-side down for the first 30 minutes then turn it over to ensure a wonderfully juicy result. Add the sherry and water and continue to cook for a further 1 hour. Do check every 20 minutes or so to make sure there is some liquid in the roasting tin and add more water, if necessary.

Once the duck is cooked, drain well and cut into quarters, removing the backbone. Place in an ovenproof dish or terracotta *cazuela*. Skim off the fat in the roasting tin, there will be plenty of it – great for roast potatoes at a later date.

Press the vegetables, along with the juices, through a *chinoise*, or sieve, or *pasapurés*, and add to the duck. Sprinkle with the prunes and toasted pine kernels and return to the oven for a further 5 minutes until piping hot.

conejo al salmorejo
rabbit in salmorejo sauce

Rabbit is extremely popular in Spain, with none of the childhood Benjamin Bunny connotations we have to contend with. Most of the farmed rabbit on offer is displayed ready paunched and skinned while the tastier wild animals are hung, fur intact, to demonstrate their origins. Never fear, once sold the specialist game dealer will have the rabbit ready for the pot in a trice.

You should begin this recipe a day in advance.

serves 4

4 garlic cloves, peeled
salt and freshly ground black
** pepper**
1 kg/2¼lb rabbit, jointed
300 ml/10 fl oz white wine
2 tbsp sherry vinegar

2 bay leaves
2 fresh sprigs of thyme
1 fresh sprig of oregano
1 tsp hot paprika
3 tbsp olive oil

Using a mortar and pestle, pound the garlic with a pinch of salt and pepper to a creamy paste.

Now place the rabbit joints in a large bowl together with the garlic paste, wine, sherry vinegar, herbs and spices. Turn the meat in the mixture and leave to marinate overnight.

Remove the rabbit from the marinade and season with a little salt. Set the marinade aside to use later.

Heat the olive oil in a large a terracotta *cazuela* or cast-iron casserole, add the rabbit and fry until golden and tender.

Pour over the marinade and simmer gently until tender. Alternatively, bake in an oven preheated to 180°C/350°F/Gas Mark 4 for about 45 minutes until tender.

Tip   This is a popular dish in the Canary Islands where it is served with *Papas Arrugadas* (see page 153). You could, of course, serve it with plain new potatoes too.

Wild or farmed?
There is no denying that wild rabbit has a much gamier, tastier flavour than its more delicate, or some would say 'bland' farmed cousin. However, as some wild animals are older they can be rather lean and tough so that an oily marinade and slow cooking are often the only way to go.

Both farmed or young wild rabbit can be grilled or roasted, but care must still be taken not to dry the lean meat out, so a few hours in an oily marinade prior to cooking is a good idea.

Wild rabbit is sold 'skin on' so that a discerning buyer can look out for the telltale sharp claws and soft ears of a young specimen.

guiso de venado
venison casserole

Having scaled the steepest, narrowest street imaginable to reach it, Cazorla's weekly market was rather an anticlimax – a mile long stretch of knickers, bath towels, pot plants and bedroom slippers and not a sausage in sight. Thankfully I was able to find some consolation at the *churros* van with a paper-full of deliciously fattening dough fritters. The view was pretty mind-blowing too, a seemingly infinite panorama of olive groves: textbook Andalucia.

With supper in mind the modest Mercado Municipal back in the town centre was a much better bet. One small butcher stocked game from the nearby Sierra – a reminder that wild boar and venison are not confined to Spain's northerly peaks, but are found in the mountainous terrain of Andalucia and Extremadura too.

Buying and cooking venison

Ciervo, or red deer, and less commonly *corzo*, roe deer, and *gamo*, fallow deer, are all available in Spain. The same tips apply to all of them.

Avoid shiny, wet looking meat that has probably not been hung for long enough, aged meat will have a dark, dull appearance.

Venison is extremely lean meat, so it has a tendency to dry out if not treated carefully.

Tender cuts such as the saddle, containing the loin and the fillet, or haunch, the leg, can be seared or roasted quickly and left quite pink.

Meanwhile, the neck and shoulder require long, slow cooking such as braising or stewing to tenderize the tougher meat. A wine marinade may help to tenderize the meat, but the down side is that it may draw out valuable moisture from the meat too, so I wouldn't bother. Adequate ageing and a very low oven temperature will do the trick.

serves 4

1 kg/2¼ lb venison, cut into large dice
salt and freshly ground black pepper
4 tbsp olive oil
100 g/ 4 oz *panceta* or fatty bacon, cubed

2 onions, diced
2 leeks, sliced and rinsed
2 carrot, peeled and diced
3 garlic cloves, crushed
1 fresh sprig of thyme
2 bay leaves
200 ml/7 fl oz red wine

Preheat the oven to 150°C/300°F/Gas Mark 2.

Season the venison with salt and pepper. Heat the olive oil in a large pan, add the venison in small batches and fry briefly, so that it sears rather than stews. Remove the meat with a slotted spoon and set aside.

Add the *panceta*, or bacon to the pan together with the onions, leeks and carrot and fry until the vegetables are soft and beginning to brown.

Next add the garlic and stir until it begins to give off its inimitable aroma. Pop the venison back in the pan. Add the herbs, the wine and just enough water to cover the meat, then cover and cook in the oven until fabulously tender. This may take anything between 1½ to 3 hours.

Season with salt and pepper to taste and serve.

You may like to accompany this dish with white rice or creamy mashed potato, but I have to say that the unlikely local combination of venison casserole and chips is divine. We are not talking the spindly French variety but chunky chips of fried potato.

85

rice and pulses

Rice and dried pulses are considered little more than padding in much of the western world, accompaniments to the more highly prized meat or fish. Not so in Spain, where top quality beans, chickpeas, lentils and rice command high prices and play a key role in many celebrated regional dishes.

Paella is, without a doubt, Spain's most famous dish, the stereotypical holiday feast served along with a jug of *sangría*. But, when tourists expect heaps of shellfish, chicken or meat with a little tasty rice to soak up the juices they are missing the point. The rice is the star of the show here. It must be well flavoured, firm and yet moist, but on no account sticky, and ideally a little crunchy and caramelized on the bottom of the pan. Cooking the *paella* is often male territory with plenty of testosterone fuelled competition but, magic touches and family secrets apart, what every cook will agree

on is the need for the right rice. Many market stalls, particularly those of Mediterranean Spain, stock a few different varieties of the short-grain *paella* rice – *Bahía* rice from the Ebro delta, the *Senia* variety from Valencia and the more expensive *Bomba* grain from Calasparra, grown increasingly in the other regions too. Locals are typically vehement about the superiority of their own local grain but even a *Valenciano* will concede that *Bomba* rice is more forgiving and less likely to end up as a stodgy mess in the hands of a novice. Smaller quantities of long-grain rice are sold too; ideal for salads, a quick supper topped with tomato sauce and fried egg or the festive dish of *Moros y Cristianos* (see page 96).

Beans are given cult status in the maritime regions of the North, where many of the varieties first arrived from the Americas. The legume stall in Santander's covered market resembles a pick-and-mix sweet

counter with over 30 varieties of legume on offer. Discerning shoppers run their hands through the beans; they should feel shiny and soft with no hint of a wrinkle. 'Son todas nuevas', they are all new season, the labels reassure, since contrary to popular belief a bean does have a shelf life. Bean lovers check for any signs of discoloration around the eye or hilum of the bean, a sign of oxidization and poor quality. Green beans from Llanes, red beans from Guerníka, black beans from Tolosa – each region has its bean and each bean a specific dish. Beans and pulses were once known as the 'carne de los pobres', the meat of the poor. Today nothing could be further from the truth, with the buttery, white Fabes de la Granja of Asturias fetching well over 10 Euros a kilo.

Chickpeas and lentils, the cornerstones of the old Spanish kitchen, are also subject to much predilection, particularly in Castille and Andalucia. Keen cooks will certainly expect a good selection for their precious Cocidos, or stews (see page 88). Who would believe you could be choosy about a chickpea? Well, a southerner will probably plump for his local Garbanzo Andaluz, a monster of a chickpea with plenty of flavour. Meanwhile, in Castille the more subtle qualities of the Garbanzo Castellano, with its almost indiscernible skin, are preferred. Certain lentils enjoy celebrity status too, the green Lenteja de la Armuña with its buttery texture and the smaller, brown Pardina renowned for its delicate taste.

Freshly cooked beans and pulses are available in larger city markets too, ideal for their fast-lane customers with no time for all that soaking and slow cooking – a boon for the more forgetful among us, who always seem to remember tonight's beans over breakfast.

cocido madrileño
madrid's feast in a pot

Many foreigners mistakenly consider Valencia's *paella* as Spain's signature dish, but ask a local and he will almost certainly herald the *cocido* as the nation's most traditional feast; a meal of chickpeas, meat and vegetables cooked in a flavoursome broth – three courses in one pot. Every area of Spain has its own local rendition (see opposite) but the king of the castle is undoubtedly the *Cocido Madrileño*.

Until recent times the *cocido* was an everyday dish, sometimes little more than chickpeas flavoured with a ham bone, an old boiling chicken and a few vegetables with meatier versions confined to the more affluent households. Nowadays time is precious, we are all on the run and the notion of the lady of the house taking a day to source and prepare the family meal is long gone. The *cocido* has risen to new heights, a dish for high days and holidays.

You will need to soak your chickpeas overnight.

serves 6–8

3 litres/5 pints water
750 g/1½ lb beef or veal shin or 500 g/1 lb 2 oz chuck steak, in one piece, and a beef bone
1 knuckle of *jamón Serrano*, or any unsmoked ham, with a little meat still attached
100 g/4 oz *jamón Serrano*, gammon works well outside Spain, in 1 piece
200 g/7 oz of bacon or belly pork, in 1 piece
1 whole head of garlic
2 bay leaves
500 g/1 lb 2 oz chickpeas, soaked overnight

3 carrots, peeled and chopped into large chunks,
3 leeks, trimmed, cleaned, chopped
2 sticks celery, chopped
1 onion, peeled, halved and stuck with 2 cloves
1 chicken, jointed into 8 pieces
200 g/7 oz cooking *chorizo* (see page 49), left in whole links
4 medium potatoes, peeled and cut in half
200 g/7 oz *morcilla*, or black pudding
200 g/7oz swiss chard, spinach or cabbage
200 g/7 oz *fideos*, *vermicelli*, or other tiny pasta

Regional variations

The *cocido* appears, in one guise or another, all over the country – a pot of chickpeas or beans, ham bones and whatever the local larder has to offer.

The famous *Cocido Maragato* of León is a carnivore's delight packed with lamb, cured beef and pork. It is topped with dumplings made from breadcrumbs and stock.

Andalucia's *Puchero* replaces much of the meat with more economical vegetables such as pumpkin, courgettes and beans.

Mallorca's *Sopa i Bullit* uses local lamb instead of beef and is flavoured with *sobrasada*, a paprika and pork paste.

The Catalan *Escudella i Carn de Olla* includes fresh *butifarra* sausages and pork meatballs flavoured with cinnamon.

Once you reach the North coast chickpeas are replaced by the celebrated local beans Galicia has its *Pote Gallego*, Asturias its *Fabada*, Cantabria the *Cocido Montañés* and The Basque Country *Potaje de Alubias* (see page 91).

Pour the water into a large pot, add the beef, the ham bone, the ham, the bacon, the head of garlic and the bay leaves, then bring to the boil, skimming off any of the grey foam as it comes to the surface.

Drain the chickpeas and add to the pot together with the carrots, leeks, celery and onion. Purists will add the chickpeas in a muslin bag or net so that they can be removed easily and served separately from the vegetables. I have never felt the need to. Ensure that all the ingredients are submerged in the water, then bring to the boil and skim the foam away again. Continue to cook, covered, at a steady simmer. Topping up with hot water as necessary.

(continues above right)

After an hour add the chicken and the *chorizo*, and cook for about 30 minutes, or until the chickpeas are almost tender.

Add the potatoes and *morcilla* or black pudding and then after another 10 minutes the chard or cabbage. Once the potatoes are tender then your *cocido* is ready. Adjust the seasoning with salt and pepper as necessary.

Next strain off most of the stock and boil the *fideos*, or pasta until tender. This soup will be served as the starter.

Chop the beef, bacon, ham, *chorizo* and *morcilla* into serving pieces and arrange them on a platter with the chicken. Pile the chickpeas and vegetables on another dish and serve.

Optional trimmings The tiny unlaid eggs of a boiling fowl are sometimes tossed into the pot at the last minute to poach gently in the broth. These are often available in the market at the poultry stall if you are feeling adventurous.

On special occasions the *cocido* may be served with meatballs, or *pelotas*. A selection of the meat is taken from the pot, about 200 g/7 oz in total, and minced meticulously by hand or whizzed in a food processor. The mixture is seasoned with a little garlic, parsley, salt and pepper and then bound together with a couple of beaten eggs and some breadcrumbs. The *pelotas* are fried in olive oil and added to the pot for the last 10 minutes of the cooking time.

arroz a la cubana
cuban rice

This combination of white rice, tomato sauce, fried eggs and banana is suprisingly good. It makes a simple and satisfying lunch dish and is an absolute winner with children. This dish is particularly popular in Catalonia a region where flaming spiced rum and the sound of lilting sea shanties, named *Habaneras*, hark back to the days when local *émigrés* returned from Cuba.

serves 4

1 x recipe tomato sauce (see page 69 with meatballs)
250 g/9 oz long-grain white rice
4 small bananas
1 tbsp butter

1 tbsp olive or vegetable oil
4 large eggs
salt and freshly ground black pepper
pinch of sweet or hot paprika

Begin by making the tomato sauce. If you are in a hurry you could even cheat and use a jar of good quality *tomate frito*, a pre-made tomato sauce available in Spain, obviously not as good as the real thing but an absolute boon when you are rushing.

Meanwhile, cook the white rice using the foolproof method right.

Cut the bananas in half lengthways and fry in the butter at once, otherwise they will oxidize and brown. Once the bananas have coloured slightly set them aside and keep warm.

Add the oil to the pan and fry the eggs over a high heat until the yolks have just set and the whites are crisp around the edges.

Serve the rice in a mound topped with the egg and bananas and surrounded with the tomato sauce. Season with salt, pepper and paprika.

Perfect rice everytime
Place the required quantity of long-grain white rice in a measuring jug and calculate double its volume of water or stock.

Take a heavy saucepan with a tightly fitting lid and bring the liquid up to the boil with 1 tsp salt for each 250 g/9 oz of rice.

Add the rice and stir just once (frequent stirring equals sticky rice). Turn down the heat, cover and simmer gently for 12 minutes. Do not be tempted to remove the lid or, worse still, stir the rice at this stage.

Leave the rice, lid on, to rest for at least 5 minutes and up to 20 minutes so that it absorbs the steam. Fluff the rice with a fork before serving.

potaje de alubias rojas
basque red bean stew

Guernika's vibrant weekly market is packed with fabulous produce. Stalls are hung with strings of the dried red *choricero* peppers that play a vital role in many classic dishes of the Basque kitchen. There are baskets heaped with the local red beans too, which I was of course assured, are infinitely superior to the equally famous black beans of Tolosa up the road.

You will need to soak the red beans overnight.

serves 4–6

500 g/1 lb 2 oz red beans, *alubias de Guernika* or *caparrones* if possible, soaked overnight

1 bay leaf

4 tbsp olive oil

150 g/5 oz soft cooking *chorizo*, pricked with a fork

150 g/5 oz *morcilla*, or black pudding, pricked with a fork (optional)

100 g/4 oz *tocino*, or salted pork fat, use fresh belly pork fat if unavailable

1 leek, trimmed and cleaned

2 onions, 1 peeled and quartered and 1 onion, finely diced

1 green pepper, finely diced

4 garlic cloves

1 tsp sweet paprika or, better still, the flesh of 1 soaked *choricero* pepper (see page 15)

salt

8 *guindillas vascas* (see page 15), to serve

Drain the beans and place in a large saucepan with double their volume of cold water and the bay leaf. Bring slowly to the boil, skimming off any frothy scum with a ladle. Reduce the heat to a gentle simmer, adding a glass of cold water every 30 minutes (see 'shocking' on page 92).

After about an hour add half the olive oil, the meat, the leek and the onion quarters and continue to simmer and 'shock' the beans until they are tender.

Meanwhile, heat the remaining olive oil in another pan, add the diced onion and green pepper and fry until soft and beginning to brown. Add the garlic and cook until golden, then add the paprika and give everything a final stir.

Once the beans are almost ready remove the leek and onion together with a couple of ladles of beans. Transfer to a blender and process until smooth. Alternatively, chop, then mash to a paste.

Remove the *chorizo*, *morcilla*, if using, and *tocino* from the pot and cut into small pieces. Next, tip the blended beans and the fried onion mixture back into the bean pot. Taste and add salt as required, remembering that the meat may be quite salty.

Serve topped with the meat and accompanied by a couple of hot *guindillas*.

habas con marisco
beans with shellfish

This is a fabulous combination from the bean-loving province of Asturias in the North. Although locals are capable of scoffing this as a starter I would happily serve it as a one-course lunch accompanied by good bread and maybe a simple green salad. You will need to soak the beans overnight.

serves 4–6

12 raw prawns, heads and shells removed and reserved
250 g/9 oz *verdinas*/flageolet or white beans such as *fabes de la Granja*, soaked overnight
1 onion, quartered
1 bay leaf
5 tbsp olive oil

salt
2 onions, finely diced
4 garlic cloves, crushed
100 ml/3½ fl oz dry white wine
675 g/1½ lb fresh clams, cleaned (see page 21)
large pinch of saffron strands
2 tbsp fresh parsley, finely chopped

Soaking and cooking beans
The Spanish take their beans seriously; buying the best quality they can get their hands on. Try to get hold of this year's beans if possible.

Soak beans in 5 litres/9 pints of cold water per kilo of beans for 8 hours. It is best not to add salt, or salty pork products, to the beans until at least halfway through the cooking time otherwise they will toughen.

'Shocking' the beans with cold water, about a glass will do, during the cooking will help to keep the skins intact and stop the beans from breaking up.

Begin by making a prawn stock with the shells and heads (see page 20).

Drain the beans and place them in a large pan with the onion quarters, bay leaf, prawn stock and enough water to cover them. Bring to the boil and skim off any froth, then reduce the heat and simmer gently. Pour in a little cold water every 20 minutes to 'shock' the beans, making sure that they are just covered with liquid.

After about an hour add 2 tbsp olive oil and 1 tsp salt and continue to cook the beans until they are tender, about 10–40 minutes.

Once the beans are ready, it's time to cook the shellfish.

Heat about 3 tbsp olive oil in a pan, add the diced onions and fry until translucent. Next add the garlic and, once it has turned golden, add the prawns. Cook for a matter of moments until they firm up, then remove from the heat.

Pour the wine into a large pan with a lid and bring to the boil. Add the clams and cover the pan. Give it a little shake from time to time, until the shells all open. Discard any that remain closed.

Shuck half of the clams and leave the rest in their shells. If the pan juices look gritty, and some clams can be very sandy, then you will need to strain the liquid.

Now it is time to put the dish together. Add the clam liquid to the bean pot. Grind the saffron and a pinch of salt in a mortar with a pestle, then add to the beans together with half of the parsley. Stir in the prawns, onions and garlic together with all the clams and simmer the beans for a minute. Check the seasoning, sprinkle with the remaining parsley and leave to stand for a few minutes before serving.

lentejas con alcachofas
lentils with artichokes

This is comfort food at its best. Lentils are quick and easy to prepare with none of the soaking time required by other pulses, and they also make an immensely satisfying dish when combined with a touch of pork fat, be it bacon or *chorizo*, or in this case both.

The addition of artichokes gives an everyday supper dish a bit of pizzazz. Some cooks will add the artichokes directly to the pot but, since lentils are famously unpredictable, their cooking time ranging from 20 minutes to an hour, this could be a recipe for disappointingly soggy artichokes. I would rather cook the artichokes and potato apart.

Lentil know-how
Look out for the tiny, dark *pardinas* or larger *lentejas de Armuña* from Castilla y León.

Brown or green lentils will hold their shape and so are ideal for stews, salads and side dishes while red lentils break down to a soft soupy consistency.

Lentils require no soaking unless you wish to reduce their cooking time, about 3 hours immersed in cold water will give you an approximately 15-minute lentil.

Do not salt lentils until they are cooked, or the skins may toughen.

Bay leaves, cumin, aniseed, cloves or thyme are common seasonings, not only do they taste good they are reputed to reduce the wind factor too.

serves 4–6

4 tbsp olive oil
2 onions, diced
1 carrot, peeled and finely diced
2 tomatoes, peeled, de-seeded
   and chopped
4 garlic cloves, crushed
100 g/3 oz hot or sweet soft cooking
   chorizo (see page 49), diced
150 g/5 oz *panceta ahumada*, or
   smoked bacon

450 g/1 lb brown lentils
1 tsp ground cumin
4 medium artichokes, prepared
   with 2 lemons (see page 142)
   and quartered
1 potato, cut into bite-sized pieces
salt and freshly ground black
   pepper
splash of extra virgin olive oil

Heat the olive oil in a large pan, add the onions and carrot and cook until soft. Next add the tomatoes, garlic, *chorizo* and *panceta* or bacon and continue to cook until the pan is swirling with the red *chorizo* fat.

Add the lentils and cumin, stirring to coat in the oil, then add enough water to completely cover the lentils. Bring to the boil then reduce the heat to a simmer and cook stirring from time to time until the lentils are soft and cooked through. You may need to add a little water to the pan from time to time to keep the lentils covered. The idea is to finish up with something that can be spooned rather than poured.

Meanwhile, place the prepared artichoke quarters and the potatoes in a separate saucepan of boiling salted water and boil for 15–20 minutes until they are tender.

Stir the artichokes into the cooked lentils, season with salt and pepper and serve with a good splash of extra virgin olive oil.

Variations   For a quicker option the lentils are fabulous without the artichokes too.

Simply boiled artichokes and potatoes make a fabulous starter, especially using tiny, new potatoes. Serve with lashings of extra virgin olive oil, salt, plenty of black pepper and a sprig of fresh parsley or thyme.

olla gitana
gypsy stew

Having driven for hours through the Andalucian Sierras to reach Cádiar, we were greeted by a Women's Institute-style jam and chutney stall. The British expats had moved in big time. Now, I have nothing against a few Brits abroad, but I was on a quest for local flavour. Thankfully, after a lively chat at the vegetable stall, a very generous Señora Lopez shared this wonderful recipe with me. The dish is in fact from the neighbouring province of Murcia, but different renditions of this vegetarian hotpot are common all over the south. You may like to substitute the pears with parsnips, as they do in Murcia when ripe pears are unavailable. You will need to soak your pulses overnight.

serves 8

450 g/1 lb chickpeas or white beans, or a mixture of both, soaked overnight or 2 x 400 g/14 oz cans chickpeas or beans
4 tbsp olive oil
4 garlic cloves, peeled but left whole
2 onions, diced
1 red pepper, diced
2 tomatoes, grated (see page 152)
1 tsp sweet non-smoked paprika
pinch of hot paprika
300 g/10 oz potatoes, peeled and cut into 5 cm/2 inch pieces
1 bay leaf
1 litre/1³/₄ pints vegetable or chicken stock

300 g/10 oz pumpkin or butternut squash, peeled, de-seeded and cut into 5 cm/2 inch pieces
200 g/7 oz green beans, topped and tailed and cut into 2.5cm/1 inch lengths
4 Conference pears, peeled, cored and chopped
salt and freshly ground black pepper
2 tbsp almonds, roasted (see page 102)
2 tbsp white wine vinegar
pinch of saffron strands, crumbled and steeped in hot water for 10 minutes
a few fresh mint leaves, chopped

Begin by draining the chickpeas or beans, placing them in a large pot and covering them with water. Bring to the boil before reducing the heat to a simmer and cooking for about an hour until they are tender. You may leave this step out altogether if using canned pulses.

Meanwhile, heat the olive oil in a large pan, add the garlic and fry until golden. Remove the garlic and set aside.

Next, using the same oil, fry the onions and red pepper until soft. Add the tomatoes and cook until reduced before adding the paprika.

Drain the chickpeas or beans and add the onion mixture, the potatoes, bay leaf and stock to the pot. Simmer for about 10 minutes, then add the pumpkin, beans and pears and continue to cook until everything is tender.

While the vegetables are cooking pound the reserved garlic, 1 tsp salt and the almonds together in a mortar with a pestle. Add the vinegar and saffron and work to a paste.

Once the vegetables are ready stir in the paste, season with salt and pepper to taste and sprinkle over a little chopped mint.

94

moros y cristianos
rice and beans

Once a year grown men reach into the dressing up box for gaudy turbans, shiny helmets, swords and blunderbusses. Gunpowder and cigar smoke fill the air. It is April, and towns all over Valencia's Levante region stage mock battles to commemorate the Christian re-conquest of Spain: the festival of *Moros y Cristianos*. The black beans and white rice supposedly represent the opposing factions. In fact they complement each other very well, just as the Moors and Christians had done for many centuries before the Catholic purging of Spain. You will need to soak your beans overnight.

serves 4

for the Moors
300 g/10 oz black beans, soaked overnight and then drained
1 bay leaf
juice and zest of 1 orange
1 tsp hot or sweet paprika
2 tbsp olive oil
1 onion, finely diced
1 green pepper, finely diced
3 garlic cloves, finely sliced
2–3 tomatoes, peeled and chopped
salt and freshly ground black pepper

for the Christians
3 tbsp olive oil or butter
1/2 onion, finely chopped
225 g/8 oz long-grain rice
600 ml/1 pint vegetable stock, chicken stock or a mixture of wine and water
1 tsp fresh thyme, chopped

to garnish
1 large sprig of fresh parsley, chopped
1 orange, peeled, cut into segments
2 tbsp extra virgin olive oil

Begin with the Moors. Place the beans in a large pan with the bay leaf, cover with water and boil for 10 minutes. Reduce the heat and continue to simmer for about 1 1/2 hours, or until the beans are tender. You may need to top up the water from time to time. Once cooked, drain the beans and stir in the orange juice, zest and paprika.

Next, heat the olive oil in a pan, add the onion and green pepper and fry until soft. Add the garlic and when you can smell the garlic cooking add the tomatoes and cook for a further 10 minutes.

Stir the onion mixture in with the beans and season with salt and pepper to taste. Reheat over a medium heat once you are ready to serve.

Now for the Christians. It is time to cook the rice. Heat the olive oil or butter in a pan, add the onion and fry until soft. Add the rice and stir well to coat the grains with the oil.

Boil the stock or water and wine in another saucepan, and add to the rice with the thyme and a pinch of salt. Cook, covered, until the rice is tender and the liquid has been absorbed, about 15 minutes. If the rice seems a little firm just add another 100 ml/ 3 1/2 fl oz water and return to the heat until it is absorbed..

Garnish the beans with chopped parsley and a few orange segments. Drizzle with extra virgin olive oil and serve with the rice (see above for presentation tips).

Presentation
To serve, you could just mound the beans in the centre of a platter and tip the rice around the edge. However, many households favour a more fancy presentation for this *fiesta* dish. You will need to grease a ring mould and pack the rice into it. It may be worth cooking 400 g/14 oz of rice in 1 litre/ 1 3/4 pints stock to ensure you have enough rice to fill the mould. Next invert the rice onto a large platter and place the beans in the centre.

Variation
This is a very satisfying vegetarian dish although you could add *jamón* to the beans to pacify more resolute carnivores.

paella valenciana
the original paella

Where better to glean an authentic recipe for the traditional *paella,* than Valencia's *Mercat Central*? After a full scale debate, all I could conclude was that fish and shellfish are absolutely out of the question, pork and duck had a large question mark hanging over them and snails, artichokes and asparagus were optional extras. Read the tips on the right before you start.

serves 6

3–4 tbsp olive oil
1 red pepper, cut into strips
1 small chicken, jointed into bite sized pieces, or better 4 chicken legs, jointed
½ a rabbit, jointed into bite-sized pieces
salt
3 garlic cloves, crushed
1 tsp sweet non-smoked paprika
2 tomatoes, peeled and diced
1 litre/1¾ pints water
24 snails, cleaned (optional)

400 g/14 oz green beans or small runner beans, *Rotjet* and *Ferraura* are popular local varieties
400 g/14 oz fresh *garrafón*, or butter beans, you could use cooked, dried beans or fresh broad beans instead
large pinch of saffron strands, soaked in a little hot water
400 g/14 oz Spanish *paella* rice
a few sprigs of fresh rosemary

Heat the olive oil in a pan, add the red pepper strips and fry until they have softened. Set aside for the garnish later.

Season the chicken and rabbit pieces with a pinch of salt and fry in the same oil until golden brown. This browning is vital to the taste of the *paella* so you will need to be patient and put up with the spitting olive oil. A pair of long kitchen tongs come in handy.

Add the garlic and, once it begins to colour, sprinkle in the paprika. Now give everything a quick stir before adding the tomato. Cook for 5 minutes until its juices have evaporated.

Add about half of the water together with the snails, if using, and all the beans. Simmer for about 15 minutes until the chicken and rabbit are cooked through and the beans are tender.

Stir in the saffron, the rice and a pinch of salt. Next pour in the remaining water. The ingredients should be completely submerged, so you may have to add a little extra water. Now, without stirring, cook over a high heat for 10 minutes, then reduce the heat and simmer for a further 10 minutes.

Check that the rice is just about cooked, if it is still firm you may need to add a splash more water and continue to cook for a couple more minutes.

Garnish with the reserved pepper strips and rosemary sprigs and cover with foil or a cloth, some still swear by a newspaper. Leave to stand for 10 minutes and then serve.

Paella know-how
The right texture will only be achieved using short-grain rice. Look out for the high quality Spanish rice from Calasparra.

A large flat pan is imperative to cook a successful *paella*. The rice should be in an even, shallow layer before the stock is added. A *paella* pan with a 40 cm/16 inch base will feed 6–8 people.

Your pan must be completely flat (I have witnessed pedantic cooks use spirit levels) and cooked over an even heat; ideally the coals of a fire or barbecue, a griddle or very large gas ring. If you are using 2 smaller rings you will need to turn the *paella* regularly to cook evenly.

As a general rule just over double the volume of stock to rice will give a good result. The rice should be almost cooked through when you leave it to rest. If the rice seems very firm just add a few tablespoons of stock and simmer for a couple of minutes longer.

Do not stir the rice – this is not a risotto, and the crispy browned, rather than burnt crust on the bottom of the pan, the *socarrat*, is absolutely delicious.

paella marinera
seafood paella

Although the *paella* originated as a peasant dish inland, flavoured with whatever the household could muster (see *Paella Valenciana,* page 97), for most of us its mere mention conjures up a mouth-watering vision of exotic shellfish atop saffron rice.

Purists would name any rice dish, bar the true Valenciana, an *arroz*, while most Spaniards happily use the term *paella* for any of the traditional rice dishes cooked in the flat, two handled pan of the same name.

Do include any of the steaming juices from the molluscs in your fish stock, the rice will only ever be as good as the stock it is cooked in.

serves 6

6 tbsp olive oil	1 tsp sweet paprika
6 tiger prawns	large pinch of saffron strands
6 *cigalas*, or langoustines/Dublin bay prawns	salt and freshly ground black pepper
500 g/1 lb 2 oz squid, cleaned and cut into small squares	1 litre/1³/₄ pints fish stock or shellfish stock (see pages 20 or 34)
½ medium onion, diced	450 g/1 lb fresh mussels, cleaned and steamed open (see page 22)
4 garlic cloves, crushed	450 g/1 lb fresh clams, cleaned and steamed open (see page 21)
2 ripe tomatoes, peeled and diced	
400 g/14 oz Spanish *paella* rice	

Consult the *paella* tips on page 97 before you begin.

Heat the olive oil in a *paella* pan, or the widest pan you own, add the prawns and langoustines and fry briefly until they colour. Set aside.

Add the squid to the pan and fry briefly, until it turns opaque, then add the onion and continue cooking until it softens. Next stir in the garlic and once you can smell the garlic, add the tomatoes. When the moisture has evaporated add the rice together with the paprika.

Grind the saffron, salt and pepper together in a mortar with a pestle and add to the rice. Pour in the stock, give everything a last stir and bring to the boil. Cook over a high heat for 10 minutes. Reduce the heat and simmer for a further 5 minutes before adding the prawns, langoustines, mussels and clams. Simmer for a further 5 minutes, then cover lightly with foil or a cloth.

Leave the rice to stand for at least 10 minutes before serving. The grains of rice on the surface may seem a little firm but they will plump up while the rice is resting.

Variation For a seafood *fideuà*, a kind of pasta *paella*, substitute the rice with 500 g/1 lb 2 oz *fideos*, a short pasta about the thickness of Italian *vermicelli* or thin spaghetti, broken into small pieces. You will require a little more stock about 1.5 litres/2½ pints in total. The pasta will only take half the time to cook, so add your shellfish to the pan after about 5 minutes. Once the pasta is cooked and has absorbed all the stock leave the pan to rest for 5–10 minutes before serving.

groceries

Floor to ceiling cans and jars; the grocer seems to spend half his life teetering up a stepladder plucking items from the top shelf. The *tienda de comestibles* or *ultramarinos* holds the contents of an average shop in a space no bigger than a wardrobe. The variety of stock is often astounding, especially in smaller markets where, as well as the customary canned foods and preserves, you may also find dried fruit and nuts, olives, pickles and spices.

Canned foods, *conservas*, so often regarded as second-class substitutes for the 'real thing', enjoy a high reputation in Spain. Shellfish is a prime example. Mussels, Venus clams, razor clams and cockles are stacked high on the shelves in their slim colourful cans. Even coastal dwellers tuck into them with gusto along with a glass of wine or sherry; they are considered to have an entirely different taste and texture from their fresh counterparts. When it comes to fish, the cured anchovies from both Catalonia and Cantabria have their passionate followers. Meanwhile, the cans of white albacore tuna, *bonito del Norte*, can make the fishmonger seem cheap. Preserved vegetables such as white asparagus, artichokes, beans and tomatoes are great store-cupboard standbys while *piquillo* peppers are an absolute must; ideal for stuffing with whatever comes to hand as a fabulous starter.

Oil and vinegar are key ingredients to snap up, especially if the stall has a selection of the local brew. Many Spanish olive oils lack the chichi packaging of their Italian or French neighbours, but customers know their stuff and have no problem buying top quality oils in huge cans or unlikely looking plastic jerry cans. Large quantities of second pressing, *Aceite*

de Oliva, are purchased for cooking and frying, while the more expensive *Aceite de Oliva Virgen Extra* is usually reserved for using raw. Excellent wine and sherry vinegar is available too for everyday salad dressings and pickles.

Salazones y encurtidos, pickles and cures, often occupy their own stall, particularly in Andalucia, the world's largest olive grove. Vast pots of table olives, predominantly green, sit side by side. They each look remarkably similar to the unenlightened but locals all have a favourite. Some are stuffed with almonds, garlic, peppers or anchovies while others are quite simply pickled in brine. Capers, gherkins, onions and sweet pickled peppers, *guindillas*, all make excellent nibbles, or accompaniments to cured meats.

Spices are often sold loose by weight – cumin and cinnamon, part of the Moorish legacy, are particularly popular. Strings of dried peppers, the sweet round *ñoras* and larger *choriceros*, festoon the walls of the stall, ready for sauces and stews. In Murcia's municipal market an entire stand is devoted to selling the quaint little cans of local paprika, and the costly saffron, so key to the regional rice dishes, is painstakingly weighed out on miniature scales.

Autumn brings in a new stock of nuts. Almonds and hazelnuts from the terraces of Mediterranean Spain are toasted and eaten just as they are, or are used for sweets and sauces. In the north, freshly gathered chestnuts and walnuts are sold straight from the sack. Dried fruit such as the favourite apricots, commonly known as *orejones*, or 'big ears', figs and prunes make great accompaniments for seasonal game while Elche dates and Málaga raisins are ideal for simple desserts.

almendras saladas
salted almonds

The terraced hillsides of Mediterranean Spain take on a magical air in early spring, veiled in a lace of almond blossom. The nuts are collected in late summer and will keep for months in their shells. They are a key ingredient in both sweet and savoury dishes, but one of the best ways to eat an almond is surely this one; simply roasted and salted, accompanied by a glass of chilled dry sherry.

Almonds have recently been hailed as one of the great antioxidants, packed with vast quantities of Vitamin E, so there's a good reason to eat double the quantity and feel no guilt at all.

makes a small bowlful
250 g/9 oz whole, blanched almonds

1 tsp salt
1 tsp olive oil

Preheat the oven to 180°C/350°F/Gas Mark 4.

Place the almonds on an oven tray and roast for 10–15 minutes, or until golden.

Meanwhile, pound the salt to a fine powder in a mortar with a pestle. Toss the roasted almonds in the salt and olive oil and return to the oven for a minute or two. Remove from the oven and leave to cool. The almonds will crisp up once cool.

Tip   You may like to add a pinch of hot or sweet smoked paprika with the salt.

pasta de aceitunas negras
black olive paste

Black olive and anchovy paste has been popular around the Mediterranean since the time of the Romans. It is particularly good with toast or quail's eggs as an aperitif or served with grilled white fish or lamb as a main course.

makes a small pot
20 black olives, stoned
6 anchovies in oil, drained
2 tbsp capers
3 garlic cloves, roughly chopped

1 tsp French mustard
leaves from a sprig of fresh thyme
4 tbsp extra virgin olive oil
salt and freshly ground black pepper

Place the olives, anchovies, capers, garlic, mustard and thyme in a blender and blitz to a rough paste, then with the motor running, gradually add the olive oil. Taste and season. You may not need salt if the anchovies or capers are particularly salty.

Buying and storing nuts
Nuts can turn rancid in a matter of weeks once they are shelled, so purchase them in small quantities from a supplier with a good turnover. Buying whole nuts is the best idea since exposure to air is the great enemy. Then you can chop, flake or process them yourself as and when you need them.

Blanched nuts keep much better than roasted, so roasting your own nuts is worthwhile.

If you have large quantities of nuts keep them in an airtight container in a cool dark place, or better still in the freezer.

Buying and storing olives
Olives that are picked before they are truly ripe are green, firm and quite sharp in flavour. Black olives are the fully ripened fruit and will usually have a mellower, oily character. In general, when it comes to Spanish table olives the tastiest varieties are green. The *Manzanilla* olive is perhaps the best known. It is excellent bought ready-stuffed with anchovies or peppers. Huge *Gordal* or *Sevillana* olives are wonderful with almonds while the tiny green to purple *Arbequina* olives have a mild smoky flavour and are usually eaten alone. However, there are reputedly over 200 varieties of olive grown in Spain, so do experiment – buy them loose from the market stall and do ask to taste first.

Once purchased the best way to keep olives for any length of time is to cover them with olive oil. Feel free to spice them up by adding chillies, dried spices, bay leaves and citrus zest to the oil.

Canary Island mojos

There are countless varieties of *mojo*, or sauce, in the Canary Islands; the most well-known are the spicy red *mojo picón* and the fresh green *mojo verde*. Visitors usually come across these served with the traditional wrinkly potatoes (see page 153), but they often accompany simple fish or meat dishes too. *Illustrated on page 103.*

mojo picón
hot red pepper sauce

Fabulous with *Papas Arrugadas* (see page 153), grilled sardines, salt cod or red meat.

serves 4–6

1/4 –1/2 dried chilli, de-seeded
1 tsp hot non-smoked paprika
1/2 tsp cumin seeds
a pinch of salt
3 garlic cloves
150 ml/5 fl oz extra virgin olive oil
50 ml/2 fl oz red wine vinegar

Grind the chilli, paprika, cumin and salt together in a mortar with a pestle. Add the garlic and crush the mixture to a paste before adding the olive oil and vinegar. You may need to do this in a separate bowl if your mortar is not the large Spanish variety.

Give everything a good stir, adjusting the oil, vinegar and salt to taste. If you are serving this sauce with the wrinkly potatoes you will definitely not need to add any more salt.

Tip   Breadcrumbs soaked in a little vinegar may be added to thicken the sauce.

mojo verde
coriander sauce

This sauce makes a wonderful accompaniment to simply grilled fish or *Papas Arrugadas* (see page 153).

serves 4–6

a pinch of salt
1 tsp cumin seeds, toasted
  6 garlic cloves, sliced
  2 tbsp fresh coriander, chopped
1–2 fresh green chillies, optional
6 tbsp extra virgin olive oil
2 tbsp white wine vinegar

Grind the salt and cumin to a powder in a mortar with pestle. Add the garlic and pound to a paste, before adding the coriander and chillies. Once you have a fairly smooth sauce stir in the olive oil and vinegar, tasting and balancing the sauce as you go.

Variation   You may like to mash a ripe avocado into the sauce or substitute the coriander with parsley. There are no hard and fast rules when it comes to a mojo.

xató
romesco salad dressing

There is certain risk involved with including this controversial recipe. Half a dozen towns between Barcelona and Tarragona defiantly claim it as their own, each with a slightly different rendition. I am bracing myself for letters of disapproval from the *Mestres Xatonaires*, Master *Xató* Makers, of Vilanova or the *Ambaixador de la Ruta del Xató*, the *Xató* Route Ambassador, contesting the presence of the hazelnut or the exclusion of the chilli, and as for using a blender… Well, here you have it, my favourite take on the *xató* sauce.

serves 4–6

½ head of garlic	**2 tsp sweet non-smoked paprika**
2 tomatoes	**1 slice of white bread, toasted**
100 g/4 oz blanched almonds	**6 tbsp red wine vinegar**
50 g/2 oz hazelnuts, blanched	**large pinch of salt**
6 *ñoras* peppers (see page 15) or	**150 ml/5 fl oz extra virgin olive oil**

Preheat the oven to 180°C/350°F/Gas Mark 4.

Place the garlic cloves (skin on) and tomatoes on a baking tray and roast for about 20 minutes until just beginning to soften. Set aside to cool. The almonds and hazelnuts can toast at the same time, on a separate tray. They will take anything between 10–15 minutes to turn golden. Do take care, burnt nuts taste bitter and these should be lightly toasted. Leave to cool.

Meanwhile, place the *ñoras* peppers, if using, in a small pan of boiling water and simmer for 10 minutes.

Toast the bread and soak it in the vinegar.

Now it is finally time to make the sauce – use a large mortar and pestle or a blender (see below). Squeeze the garlic from the skins and pound to a smooth paste with a large pinch of salt. Add the nuts and continue to work with the pestle until they are finely ground.

Cut open the peppers and scrape out the thin layer of flesh from under the skin, add to the nuts with 2 tbsp of the cooking water. If you are using paprika instead, then now is the time to add it with a little water. Continue to pound until the sauce becomes smooth and velvety.

Slowly add half the olive oil, as if you were making a mayonnaise, stirring all the time, then break the soaked bread into small pieces and pound into the sauce. Finally, add the remaining olive oil, continuing to stir as you go. You should have a thick, creamy sauce.

And, if this all seems too much like hard work, you could throw caution to the wind. Toss everything, but the olive oil into the blender and whiz until smooth, then with the motor running, gradually add the oil until you have your deliciously velvety sauce.

Check the seasoning, the sauce should taste sharp – you may need more vinegar. Serve as a salad dressing

Traditional *xatonada* salad
Huge crowds gather in local town squares around Tarragona at Carnival time to eat a traditional salad with the delicious *xató* dressing.

Here is a quick throw-together salad recipe to serve four:
One head of curly endive, a large 200 g can of tuna, 12 salted anchovies, a large handful of *Arbequina* olives, or other tasty black olives such as the French *Niçoise* and 2 boiled eggs, all topped with the *xató* sauce. The real thing has strips of salt cod too. Do add some if you'd like (see page 44) and halve the number of anchovies.

Tip
This dressing makes a fabulous accompaniment to prawns, simply grilled fish, asparagus and the local speciality of *calçots* (see page 140).

dátiles rellenos
stuffed dates

Fabulous with a strong *café solo* or espresso, these extremely sweet and sensual little treats will transport you to the realms of the Moorish sultans. You could replace the walnuts with almonds or pistachios too.

makes 24-30

100 g/4 oz shelled walnuts
2 tbsp honey
24-30 fresh or dried dates, stoned

Process the walnuts with a hand-held blender or in a small food processor just until you have a very rough powder. Mix the nuts with the honey to a stiff paste and place in the refrigerator for a couple of hours to firm up.

Take small spoonfuls of the paste and stuff into the cavity of each date. These will keep for a couple of weeks in a covered container in a cool, dry place.

dátiles con beicon
dates with bacon

These sweet and savoury nibbles are often known as *delicias de Elche*, or delights from Elche, as the town is home to the only date plantation in Europe; not that I would know – I somehow managed to navigate my way into the town centre without spotting a single palm. A bemused girl in the tourist office looked on with a mixture of disbelief and disdain as I enquired upon their whereabouts. Needless to say from that point on there seem to be a palm tree at every turn.

makes 12

12 fresh or dried dates
12 roasted almonds (see page 102)
6 rashers of streaky bacon

Preheat the oven to 200°C/400°F/Gas Mark 6.

Remove the date stones and replace each with a roasted almond.

Using the back of a knife against a chopping board, stretch the bacon rashers. Now cut the rashers in half and wrap around each date, securing with a cocktail stick.

Place the dates in an oven tray and bake for about 10 minutes, or until the bacon is cooked through and beginning to brown. Serve hot.

tortada de almendra
almond cake

This cake from Murcia in the Southeast is similar to Galicia's *Tarta de Santiago* apart from the zesty sugar syrup that is poured over the cake once cooked. A touch of rum, brandy, Cointreau or sweet sherry could be added to the syrup for a more adult version.

You could leave out the syrup altogether for a lighter cake, which would make a great dessert served with tart fresh fruit such as raspberries or apricots, or the cherry compote on page 165.

Grind your own nuts
The flavour of your cake, or any other dish for that matter, will be so much fresher if you purchase whole, blanched almonds and grind them yourself. Just place the nuts in a food processor, brace yourself for a hideous racket and pulse until you have a fine powder.

serves 8–10

**olive oil or butter, for oiling
  or greasing**
6 eggs, separated
200 g/7 oz caster sugar
300 g/10 oz ground almonds
**60 g/2½ oz plain flour, sifted
  with 1 tsp baking powder
  or 60 g/2½ oz self-raising flour**

pinch of ground cinnamon
grated zest of 1 orange or lemon

for the syrup
150 g/5 oz sugar
200 ml/7 fl oz water
1 stick cinnamon
pared zest of 1 orange or lemon

Preheat the oven to 170°C/325°F/Gas Mark 3.

Line the base of a 24 cm/9 inch cake tin with baking paper and oil or grease the sides of the tin with a little olive oil or butter.

In a clean, grease-free bowl, beat the egg whites until firm, as if you were making meringues (see page 122), then slowly add half of the sugar whisking all the time.

Next, in another large bowl, whisk the remaining sugar with the egg yolks until pale and fluffy. Fold the meringue mixture into the yolks then fold in the almonds, sifted flour, cinnamon and zest. The idea is to preserve as much of the valuable air as possible.

Spoon the mixture carefully into the prepared tin and bake in the oven for about 45 minutes, or until firm to the touch and beginning to shrink away from the sides of the tin.

Meanwhile, make the syrup. Place the sugar, water, cinnamon stick and citrus zest together in a saucepan and heat slowly until the sugar has dissolved. Increase the heat and boil the mixture for about 5–10 minutes, or until thick and syrupy but by no means caramelized. Take the pan off the heat, remove the cinnamon stick and citrus zest and leave to cool.

Turn out the cake and cool on a wire rack placed over a plate. Puncture the top of the cake with a skewer and slowly pour over the syrup. Serve.

eggs and dairy

Some provincial markets still manage to draw smallholders and farmers in from the surrounding area with a couple of boxes of their own produce to sell. Home-laid eggs and misshapen artisan cheeses are always a reassuring sight – they are the signs of a truly local affair. The weekly market at Cangas de Ónis, high in the Picos de Europa mountains pulls in a huge crowd of local producers. Trestle tables are covered with tomatoes, potatoes, beans and cut flowers, as well as the fresh cheeses and baskets of eggs.

A genuine free-range egg can transform a dish such as the simple tortilla that tops the tapas menu in virtually every bar. I would never have believed how sublime that simple combination of eggs, potatoes and oil could be until I tasted a warm, juicy omelette in a Galician farmhouse. No tricks, no sorcery, just freshly laid eggs straight from the henhouse, it really was exceptional. The largest markets have entire stalls

devoted to selling vast ranges of eggs. Ous de Calaf, in Barcelona's Boquería, stocks goose, duck and ostrich eggs, the latter hollowed for decorative purposes, as well as the more customary quail and hen's eggs. And, shell-less unborn eggs from boiling fowl can be purchased at the poultry stand should you decide to throw a few in to your *Cocido*, stew (see page 88) as more traditional cooks like to do.

Eggs are combined with milk in the nation's favourite desserts – *Flan*, *Crema Catalana*, *Natillas* and *Leche Frita* (see pages 118–20). These popular custard-based desserts were confined to the North until relatively recently. The scarcity of milk in the South meant that egg yolks were combined with orange juice, in Valencia's own version of the *Flan* or, in the case of Andalucia's cholesterol hit, *tocino del cielo*, with vast quantities of sugar and water.

Galicia, Asturias and Cantabria have long been

regarded the dairy of Spain. In Santiago de Compostela, pats of butter are still sold wrapped in fresh cabbage leaves, keeping with time-honoured tradition. Local cakes and pastries are made with butter rather than the customary pig fat or olive oil used elsewhere in Spain. But, it is at the cheese counter that regional differences and localized producers really shine.

Broadly speaking cow's milk cheese is restricted to the north coast while those made from sheep's and goat's milk are available across the rest of the country. Great cheeses such as Manchego transcend regional boundaries and are available virtually anywhere in the country, or the world for that matter. Meanwhile, there are hundreds of cheeses produced in such tiny quantities that they never make it out of their own immediate area. There are 40 registered cheeses in the region of Asturias alone, and most are unknown to anyone but a local. These cheeses give regional markets their own very special magic.

A local producer had brought some of his pungent Gamonedo cheese to the market in Cangas de Ónis. Similar to the internationally renowned Cabrales it is made with a blend of cow's, sheep's and goat's milk, in proportions that vary with the seasons. I shall never forget that lightly smoked, pungent cheese. Even when you tuck into a familiar cheese it seems to taste better in situ. Cow's milk cheese is the pride of Galicia and the young, creamy Tetilla I scoffed with a hunk of rye bread at Ribávia was exceptional. It was hands above the Tetilla I buy from my deli back at home, but perhaps the romantic picnic spot in the misty vineyards had played its part too. And, as for the sheep and goat's cheeses at the June market in Cáceres, I have never seen such a spectacular selection: torture indeed for a heavily pregnant cheese lover.

mayonesa
mayonnaise

The people of Menorca will proudly insist that the name *mayonesa* is a derivation of *mahonesa*, a reference to their island capital of Mahón. What they will fail to add is that it was reputedly a displaced French chef in Mahón who, at a loss with what to serve his Duke, came up with the recipe. Whatever its origins it is a classic. Just remember to keep the mayonnaise refrigerated until you are about to serve your food, especially on a hot summer's day.

makes about 300 ml/½ pint

2 egg yolks, at room temperature (see note)
salt and freshly ground white or black pepper
lemon juice or white wine vinegar to taste
250 ml/8 fl oz olive oil – half extra virgin and half ordinary olive oil or sunflower oil

Mix the egg yolks, a pinch of salt and a few drops of lemon juice or vinegar together in a bowl.

Now add the olive oil to the yolks literally a few drips at a time to begin with and then, when at least a quarter of the oil has been absorbed, add the rest of the oil in a steady stream, whisking all the time. The mayonnaise should become thick and wobbly once you have incorporated all the oil.

Splash in a little vinegar or citrus juice, salt and a pinch of white or black pepper to taste.

Eggs and emulsions If you are using eggs straight from the refrigerator, beware, they have a tendency to curdle and so you will need to add the first few drops of oil very slowly. Do not despair if your sauce splits. Start with a fresh egg yolk in a new bowl and add the curdled mixture slowly as if you were making the mayonnaise from scratch.

allioli

Catalan purists will be surprised to find this recipe in the egg section. A true *allioli* is quite literally *all*, or garlic and *oli*, or oil, with a seasoning of lemon juice or vinegar and salt. I have even witnessed a luckless Frenchman be disqualified from an *allioli* contest for including an egg yolk. Yet most restaurants and busy cooks opt for this version, which is in truth just a very garlicky mayonnaise. It is easier to make and less likely to give you hairs on your chest.

makes about 300 ml/½ pint

2–4 garlic cloves, crushed in a press or with a little salt in a mortar with a pestle
salt and freshly ground white or black pepper
2 egg yolks, room temperature (see note above)
250 ml/8 fl oz olive oil
a splash of wine vinegar, lemon juice or Seville orange juice to taste

Mix the garlic, ½ tsp salt and egg yolks together thoroughly in a bowl.

Slowly add the olive oil to the yolks and garlic, literally a few drips at a time to begin with, and then in a steady stream, whisking all the time. The allioli should reach a shuddering jelly-like texture once you have incorporated all the oil.

Splash in a little vinegar or citrus juice, salt and a pinch of white or black pepper to taste.

Tip If you are really short of time or you are making large quantities of *allioli* for a party, then you may prefer to make this simpler version in the blender. Just use the recipe above substituting a whole egg for one of the yolks. With the motor running, steadily add the oil to the eggs and garlic. Season with vinegar, salt and pepper to taste.

tortilla española
spanish omelette

This is the quintessential Spanish dish, where everyday ingredients come together to create something truly special. Leave those rubber, vacuum-packed Frisbees to languish in the chiller cabinet, there is nothing to compare with a soft-centred home made *tortilla*.

Do not be tempted to reduce the amount of oil in the recipe – it is the key to an authentic Spanish omelette. Weight watchers need not apply!

serves 4, or 8 as *tapas*

300 ml/10 fl oz light olive oil, plus 2 tbsp extra olive oil
700 g/1¹/₂ lb waxy potatoes, peeled, cut into chips and sliced into thin squares

1 medium onion, diced (optional)
5 medium eggs
¹/₂ tsp salt

Heat the 300 ml/10 fl oz olive oil in a deep frying pan, add the potato and onion, if using, and cook the potatoes gently over a medium heat. The idea is to soften them without any colouring or burning.

After about 15 minutes, once the potatoes are cooked, drain them in a colander and reserve the oil for your next *tortilla*.

Place the eggs in a large bowl and, using a fork, beat thoroughly before stirring in the potatoes and onion, if using, and seasoning with salt.

Next heat 1 tbsp olive oil in your *tortilla* pan (see right) and as soon as it is hot add the omelette mixture. Reduce the heat to medium and cook for about 5 minutes until the bottom begins to set. Use a wooden spatula to loosen the edges of the *tortilla* and give the pan a shake.

Now for the adrenaline rush, it is time to flip your omelette. A large plate will do the job but a flat saucepan lid will make it easier giving you a handle to grip onto. Some enthusiasts own a specialist 'flipper' (see right). Invert the omelette onto the flat surface, add another tablespoon of oil to the pan and slip the tortilla back in. Continue cooking until the tortilla feels almost set – a little squashy rather than bouncy to the touch. Perfectionists will flip the omelette a couple more times during the cooking to achieve the characteristic rounded sides, but that is up to you.

Tip *Tortilla* is wonderful served while warm with a soft, oozing centre, but if you plan to leave it standing at room temperature for any length of time, it is safer to cook the eggs more thoroughly until just firm.

The key to a good *tortilla*: the right pan
A vital factor when making *tortillas* is to own the right pan, an average frying pan will result in a thin leathery omelette or, worse still, a mess welded to the base. The egg mixture should only just fit in the pan to create an authentically thick and juicy omelette.

I have a 20 cm/8 inch diameter, non-stick frying pan reserved for the purpose – it is worth investing in one if you plan to make the potato or any other thick Spanish omelette on a regular basis. And don't let those egg-frying Philistines wielding their metal spatulas anywhere near it.

If you fancy becoming a pro' you can pick up a very economical plastic disc with a handle, specifically designed for turning omelettes, from any good Spanish kitchen shop.

tortilla de espinacas
spinach tortilla

An exceptionally juicy omelette packed with healthy spinach. The mixture may seem very wet when you begin to cook it but will firm up enough to be sliced and even eaten with your fingers, if you like. The secret is to drain your spinach well, squashing out the moisture in a sieve with a wooden spoon.

serves 4, or 8 as *tapas*

500 g/1 lb 2 oz spinach, washed
   and any tough stalks removed
2 tbsp water
2 tbsp olive oil

5 medium eggs
½ tsp salt and a good grind of
   black pepper

Place the spinach and water in a saucepan with a tight-fitting lid and cook over a medium heat for a few minutes until the spinach has just wilted. Drain in a sieve, reserving the spinach juice to drink later – people pay good money for vegetable juice these days.

Heat the olive oil in a small frying pan, add the spinach and fry for a moment or two.

In a bowl, beat the eggs with the salt and pepper, then add to the spinach, stirring well to combine. The mixture should only just fit in the pan, guaranteeing a thick and juicy result.

Now cook the omelette over a medium heat until you can see the sides beginning to firm up. Loosen the edges with a wooden spatula (woe betide anyone who dares touch my precious pan with a metal one) and give the pan a shake.

Now take a large plate, flat saucepan lid or, better still, the plastic disc with a handle the Spanish have designed specifically for the job (see note on previous page) and invert the omelette. Take care as the base will still be soft and runny.

Slip the omelette back into the pan and continue to cook for a further 5 minutes until the centre feels springy, rather than soft, to the touch. Turn the *tortilla* onto a serving plate and eat hot or at room temperature.

Custard-based desserts

flan
caramel custard

Served in bars throughout Spain, these little custard puddings are all too often of the mass-produced variety. Not so in the Boqueria market's Bar Pinotxo where Albert bakes this ever-popular dessert two dozen at a time in his tiny galley-style kitchen. Cooking a lusciously creamy home-made *flan* is totally straightforward once you have mastered the simple art of making a caramel.

serves 4
for the caramel
110 g/4 oz white granulated sugar
4 tbsp water
for the custard
3 eggs

3 egg yolks
100 g/4 oz white sugar
600 ml/1 pint full fat milk
2 drops of vanilla extract

Preheat the oven to 150°C/300°F/Gas Mark 2.

Begin by making the caramel, making sure that you have 4 *flan* moulds (see page 17) or ramekins at the ready. Place the sugar and water in a small pan and warm gently over a low heat until the sugar dissolves. Do not be tempted to stir the caramel at any stage; it is best left to its own devices. Now increase the heat and boil rapidly until the sugar turns a light toffee brown. Take care not to overcook as the sugar will continue to bubble and darken once the pan is removed from the heat.

Moving swiftly, divide the caramel between the 4 moulds, by now it will have reached the perfect, deep brick-brown colour that you are after.

Now you can make the custard. Using a spoon, mix the eggs, yolks and sugar together in a large bowl.

Bring the milk to the boil in a small pan. Leave to cool for an instant before stirring into the egg mixture. Add the vanilla extract and pour the custard into the moulds.

Stand the moulds in a roasting tin, and pour in enough hot water to come halfway up their sides. Cook in the oven for about 35–40 minutes until the custard is just set. Leave to cool before refrigerating.

When you are ready to serve, run a knife around the moulds and carefully turn out the custards with their accompanying caramel syrup.

crema catalana
catalan crème brûlée

It is worth buying some of the individual terracotta dishes traditionally used for *Crema Catalana*. Their wide, shallow shape ensures just the right ratio of burnt sugar to custard. You will usually track them down in the *ferretería*, ironmongers; don't ask me why. Snap up at least a dozen as most will be instantly transformed into saucers for flowerpots, hamster food bowls or handy containers for small change and, rather frustratingly, be nowhere to be seen next time you make *Crema*.

serves 4

1 tbsp cornflour, *maizena* (cornstarch)
570 ml/1 pint full fat milk
1 stick cinnamon
pared zest of ½ lemon

4 egg yolks
3 tbsp caster sugar
4 tbsp granulated sugar, for caramelizing

Begin by mixing the cornflour to a paste and a little bit of milk in a small bowl and set aside.

Next, bring the rest of the milk, the cinnamon stick and lemon zest to the boil in a small pan. Once the milk has reached the boil, turn off the heat and leave the flavours to infuse.

Meanwhile, mix the egg yolks, caster sugar and cornflour paste together in a large bowl, then pour over the warm milk, stirring all the time.

Rinse out the milk pan and pour in the custard. Cook over a medium heat, stirring constantly until thickened. I find a square-bottomed wooden spoon very useful for this, allowing me to scrape the bottom of the pan at the same time, giving nothing a chance to stick. Do not let the custard boil – the cornflour will help to stabilize the mixture, but the custard can still become lumpy if it overheats.

Once the mixture is slightly thicker remove the pan from the heat and keep stirring for a minute or two. Straining the custard will ensure a silky smooth texture as you pour it into ramekins or shallow terracotta dishes used in Catalonia. Place the custards in the refrigerator until ready to serve.

Just before serving, sprinkle the custards with a thin layer of sugar and, using a cook's blowtorch or a very quick flash under your hottest grill, caramelize until a deep brown colour.

Tip Lovers of kitchen gadgetry can pick up a caramelizing tool designed specifically for the job. It is a type of branding iron that you place in the gas flame until red-hot and then sear the sugar with. Upmarket electric versions are available for true enthusiasts.

natillas custard
If the thought of all these caramel desserts is putting your teeth on edge then here is your answer. *Natillas* are a nursery favourite, a simple custard flavoured with cinnamon. Follow the recipe for the *Crema Catalana*, omitting the burnt sugar crust at the end. Sprinkle with a pinch of ground cinnamon instead.

For a more exotic version you may like to use orange rather than lemon zest and add a touch of orange flower water to the custard once it is made. A carefully judged hint of rosewater and a sprinkling of pomegranate seeds would make a custard fit for Moorish sultan.

For a more adult dessert hide a layer of dried fruit such as apricots, dates or figs steeped in brandy under the blanket of custard.

leche frita
fried custard

A rather unappetizing title for one of Spain's most exquisite and popular desserts, I must urge you to try it. Best served hot, the crispy sugar and cinnamon crust contrasts magically with the creamy custard centre. The zesty, lightly spiced flavour works particularly well with the caramelized oranges (see page 160), but try using a vanilla pod to infuse the milk instead – it is heaven combined with the strawberries on page 167. Begin this a few hours, or even a day in advance

(see page 160) ... on page 167

serves 4–6

butter, for greasing
3 tbsp cornflour, *maizena*
500 ml/16 fl oz full fat milk
pared zest of 1/2 a lemon
1 stick cinnamon
4 tbsp caster sugar

3 egg yolks
vegetable oil, for frying

for the coating
2 tbsp plain flour, sifted
2 eggs, beaten
2 tbsp caster sugar
1 tsp ground cinnamon

Grease a rectangular tray with butter.

Mix the cornflour to a paste with a couple of tablespoons of the milk in a small bowl and set aside.

Next, bring the rest of the milk, the lemon zest and cinnamon stick to the boil in a small pan. Once the milk has reached the boil, turn off the heat and leave the flavours to infuse.

Meanwhile, beat the sugar, eggs and cornflour paste together in a bowl until it is well combined and pale in colour.

While the milk is still warm strain it onto the egg mixture, stirring well. Rinse out the milk pan and pour in the custard. Cook, stirring constantly, until the custard thickens. I have a square-bottomed wooden spoon that is ideal for the purpose, I can scrape the bottom of the pan as I stir preventing it sticking and burning on the bottom of the pan. Reduce the heat and cook for a further 2 minutes.

Pour the custard into the prepared tray to a thickness of about at least 3 cm/1 1/4 inch. Transfer to the refrigerator to cool completely and become firm.

After a few hours turn out the custard and cut into 5 cm/2 inch triangles.

Heat enough oil for frying in a large heavy pan. A depth of oil about 3cm/1 1/4 inch is ideal.

Now you can prepare your production line. You will need a plate of flour, a dish with the beaten egg and another plate of the sugar and cinnamon mixed together. Dip the triangles first into the flour, then the beaten egg. Fry the custards until golden brown, then leave to drain on kitchen paper.

Turn the fried triangles in the sugar and cinnamon until coated and serve at once. Alternatively, place in a warm oven, 100°C/200°F/Gas Mark 1/4, until ready to serve.

Using citrus zest
Try to buy unwaxed or organic fruit whenever possible. Failing this, give the skin of the lemon or orange a good wash under very hot running water to remove some of the wax and pesticides. Make sure that the zest has as little white pith as possible, on it. It is extremely bitter and will taint the flavour of any custard or infusion.

soplillos
almond meringues

Almond blossom brings a first glimpse of spring to the mountain villages of the Alpujarras near Granada. Colourful striped blankets hang over doorways warding off the persistent chill and snow still lies thick on the peaks of the Sierra Nevada above. Later in the year the almonds are harvested, finding their way into many a dish, sweet and savoury alike.

Soplillos are a local delicacy dating back to Moorish times. These "puffs" of almond meringue range from the dry, dusty variety that seem to self destruct at the touch of a spoon to those with a deliciously chewy toffee-like centre (dental insurance recommended). This recipe will most likely produce the latter.

Storing egg whites
You may not have the time or the inclination to whip up a mountain of meringues next time you are making an egg yolk-based dish, such as *Allioli* (see page 114) or *Flan* (see page 118), but do remember that egg whites can be frozen very successfully, or refrigerated in an airtight container for up to a week. Do not worry about keeping a count for future use; an average egg white measures about 30 ml/1 fl oz/ 2 tbsp.

makes 36 small/24 medium

400 g/14 oz whole blanched almonds
6 medium egg whites
a pinch of salt

500 g/1 lb 2 oz caster sugar
zest and juice of 1 unwaxed lemon

Preheat the oven to 150°C/300°F/Gas Mark 2.

Cover 2 baking trays with silicone paper.

Bake the almonds in a roasting tin for about 10 minutes until lightly roasted. Pulse the nuts in a food processor for a few seconds, breaking them down to the size of pine kernels. I have also used flaked almonds, which give a different but equally successful texture. Take care when roasting the nuts, because they can burn in a matter of seconds. One call from the double-glazing salesman and they will be fit for the bin.

Whisk the egg whites and salt in a large clean bowl until they are stiff and snow-like. Next add half of the sugar, one spoon at a time, whisking between each addition. The meringue should become very stiff and shiny. Whisk in the lemon juice and zest.

Mix the remaining sugar and almonds together in a bowl and carefully fold the mixture into the meringue. Dab a tiny amount of the meringue between the paper and baking tray to secure the paper, then using two spoons, place dollops of the mixture onto the paper, leaving space for expansion. This will make about 36 Ping-Pong ball-sized meringues.

Place the meringues in the oven for about 25–30 minutes until pale golden and slightly cracked. It is an idea to turn the trays around after 15 minutes as few ovens have absolutely even temperatures throughout.

Tip   I love to serve these meringues with vanilla ice cream and sultanas soaked in dark, sweet Pedro Jiménez sherry.

arroz con leche
rice pudding

The generous quantity of milk required for this dish made it a Northern speciality until relatively recently, while the lack of dairy pastures in the South led to a version made with almond milk. Nowadays milk is available everywhere, although much of it of the long-life variety. I would reserve this recipe for fresh, full cream milk – dieting has no place in a dish such as this and skimmed milk will give a watery, thin result.

serves 4

1.5 litres/2½ pints full cream milk
1 stick cinnamon
pared zest of 1 lemon
110 g/4 oz pudding rice

30 g/1 oz/2 tbsp unsalted butter
55 g/2 oz caster sugar
1 tsp ground cinnamon

Bring the milk, cinnamon stick and lemon zest to the boil in a large saucepan. Watch the milk carefully as it has a terrible habit of erupting out of the pan.

Add the rice and reduce the heat as low as it will go. The dessert should barely simmer for at least 1 hour and preferably even 2 hours until soft. You will need to stir the rice occasionally to prevent it sticking to the bottom of the pan. Leave the pan uncovered allowing the milk to evaporate and giving a lusciously creamy result.

Once the rice is soft add the butter and sugar. You may decide to add more or less, a good excuse to taste as you go.

The rice is usually served cold, although there is nothing to stop you serving it warm.

Variation   Try piling a few sherry-plumped raisins and toasted flaked almonds on the top.

Tips   If your stove is too hot for long slow simmering then it may be worth purchasing a heat diffuser (see page 17). You could alternatively turn your back on tradition, be thoroughly British and bake the pudding in the oven preheated to 150°C/300°F/ Gas Mark 2 for about 3 hours. The downside is the unpleasant rubbery skin that forms on the top, but don't despair there will be some bizarre individual at the table who will relish it (there's one in every family).

flaó eivissenc
ibicenco cheesecake

You are more likely to pick up a pair of rope-soled sandals or a beaded headscarf than the weekly fruit and veg' at most of Ibiza's markets. A very welcome exception is San Joan's Saturday market; the place to fill your basket with glorious organic local produce such as oranges, almonds, honey and goat's cheese.

The rocky island is perfect goat terrain and the traditional cheesecake, *flaó*, is made with a very fresh goat's cheese giving it a deliciously sharp edge. The signature flavours of mint and aniseed work well with cow's cheese too, and the addition of a lemon juice will give the extra zing.

Cooking pastry
Place a heavy baking sheet in your oven when you switch it on. Lay the tart tin directly on top to cook. The baking sheet will conduct heat and help the base of your pastry to cook through.

serves 8

olive oil or butter, for oiling or greasing
200 g/7 oz plain flour, plus extra for dusting
a pinch of salt
½ tsp aniseed, crushed in a mortar with a pestle
5 tbsp light olive oil or vegetable oil
3 tbsp *Anis Seco*, or Pernod or Pastis
about 2–5 tbsp water
1 tbsp icing sugar, for dusting

for the filling

450 g/1 lb very fresh goat's cheese, *Mató* (see page 127), ricotta or cream cheese
200 g/7 oz granulated sugar
3–5 fresh mint leaves, finely chopped
zest and juice of 1 lemon (leave out the juice if you are using goat's cheese)
4 medium eggs, beaten

Lightly oil or grease a 24 cm/9 inch tart tin with olive oil or butter.

Sift the flour and salt together into a large bowl and stir in the oil and aniseed liquor. Add enough water to bind the mixture to a dough-like consistency. Pull the mixture together into a ball, cover with clingfilm and leave to rest for 15 minutes.

Preheat the oven to 180°C/350°F/Gas Mark 4.

Mix the cheese, sugar, mint and lemon zest and juice together in a large bowl. The speediest way is to use a food processor, but you could just use a fork. Next process or stir in the eggs until you have a well-blended mixture.

Roll out the pastry to fit the tin and add the cheese filling. Bake in the oven for 30–40 minutes until the filling is just set and the top is golden. Leave to cool before removing from the tin.

Serve the tart at room temperature, dusted with icing sugar, as a dessert or teatime snack.

selección de quesos y frutos secos
cheese and fruit platter

There are dozens of exquisite cheeses available in Spain. I have chosen a few of the most celebrated from which I would select my 'Desert Island' cheese board. Cheese is often combined with dried fruit, honey or *Dulce de Membrillo*, quince paste (see page 170), a delicious of marriage of the sweet and savoury.

Cow's milk

Mahón cheese from Menorca is soft and mild when young but wonderfully sharp and punchy once matured for at least a year (Mahón Reserva). It is ideal for grating on vegetable or pasta dishes.

Mató is a fresh Catalan cheese akin to ricotta. It is known as Requesón elsewhere in Spain. It is sometimes made with ewe's milk. This cheese is delicious served with honey and toasted pine kernels as a breakfast or dessert, and it is also used in cheesecakes.

Tetilla is a breast-shaped cheese from lush green Galicia. It is deliciously soft and creamy when young and often teamed with *Dulce de Membrillo*, quince paste (see page 170).

Mixed milk – blue cheeses

Picos de Europa or **Valdeón** is a deliciously creamy, pungent blue cow's milk cheese from the mountains of Cantabria. It sometimes contains a little goat or sheep's milk too. Serve walnuts with this cheese.

Cabrales, the king of the blues, is made from a blend of cow's, goat's and sheep's milk, the proportions varying according to the season. This cheese is often eaten when extremely blue and sharp when it is absolutely delicious accompanied with the local Asturian honey.

Sheep's milk

Idiazábal is a mildly smoked, hard cheese from the highlands of the Basque country and Navarre. It is heavenly combined with *dulce de manzana*, firm apple jelly.

Manchego is the celebrity among Iberian cheeses. The dry plains of the Meseta offer a meagre diet of herbs and grasses to the local sheep, resulting in low yields of intensely flavoured milk. The Manchego cheese is firm and caramel-like as a curado (1 year old cheese) becoming increasingly hard and peppery as it ages to an *añejo* (over 2 years old). Delicious with *Dulce de Membrillo*, quince paste (see page 170).

Torta del Casar is, in my mind, a 'one man show'. It is best served at about 20°C/68°F. A meltingly soft sheep's cheese, just slice off the top of a whole cheese and dip into the creamy interior: an instant fondue. Spoon the cheese onto lightly toasted bread.

Goat's Milk

Garrotxa is a hard cheese from Catalonia with a wonderfully smooth texture. Try serving it with walnuts or hazelnuts.

Montenebro or **Queso de Tietar** is a semi-cured firm log of nutty goat's cheese with a grey rind, from Ávila. It is fabulous served with *pan de higos*, the compressed cake of dried figs and almonds available at local markets and good delicatessens.

El Suspiro from Toledo, with its fresh, creamy charm, will even convert those who claim to hate goat's cheese. It has none of the 'farmyardy' flavour associated with goat's cheese. Delicious served with juicy sultanas.

Tip

There are no hard and fast rules when it comes to serving cheese, however, it is infinitely better to produce one exceptional cheese than a collection of small wedges. Even when entertaining keep the selection of cheeses small, otherwise the platter will look sad and decimated by the time a few people have helped themselves.

Three varieties will usually keep everyone happy: maybe one goat's, one sheep's, one cow's or one young creamy, one blue and one matured hard cheese. Allow 75–100 g/3–4 oz per person.

the bakery

The bakery is always busy. Many Spaniards buy their daily *barra de pan* and the tooting horn of the bread van is still a familiar sound in small villages that lack their own *panadería*. Bread accompanies every meal, soaking up juices and satisfying appetites, and often taking the place of the potatoes or rice that we might choose to serve. Thankfully the factory-produced sliced loaf, usually referred to as *pan bimbo*, has few followers, and is most likely to be found on the breakfast buffet at dubious hotels or in a plastic, petrol station, sandwich known as a *bikini*. Meanwhile, *pan de molde*, refers to the square-shaped loaf and, if picked up in the bakery, may be quite acceptable for cooking or sandwiches, but it is certainly not served at a meal. The Spanish loaf has a free, curvaceous form, which varies across the regions.

Most bread is white. In fact the quest for a Granary or wholemeal loaf will often lead you to a health food shop where all the poor souls with dodgy digestive systems are sent. The white bread contains little salt and stales quickly, but is often made into breadcrumbs or used to thicken soups and sauces. It is certainly worth looking out for the stalls of uneven crusty loaves that are baked in wood-fired ovens and sometimes sold in the country markets. In Catalonia the typical *pa de pagès* is a fabulously chewy loaf, with a dark crust, that keeps very well. It is heaven eaten, as *pa amb tomàquet*, with tomato flesh and olive oil, the local answer to bread and butter.

Galician bread is another story. Rye and corn replace or accompany the wheat in many traditional loaves. Once a sign of hardship, these tasty sourdough breads are now appreciated for their depth of flavour and wonderful texture. Castille is often known as the Spanish breadbasket, with its vast swathes of wheat but the average, bland white bread

can't begin to compare with the honest, hearty loaf of Galicia. Even the artisan wheat bread has its magic. The outdoor market in Ourense is a collection of bizarre little kiosks resembling beach huts or garden sheds. The local produce is fabulous but my lasting memory is the selection of incredible bread. A local speciality of rye bread studded with juicy sultanas made the most delicious picnic with some fresh Galician cow's milk cheese.

Snacks can be picked up at the baker's in some regions. The *Empanada*, a Galician flat pie, is fast food at its best. It is available by the slice and stuffed with anything from cockles to spiced pork. Meanwhile, in Catalonia and the Balearic Islands they have the *Coca*, rather like a pizza but eaten cold. *Coques* can be sweet or savoury, or, as in the case of the sugar and pork crackling variety, a combination of the two. *Bollos preñados*, or pregnant buns, are an

Asturian invention, a loaf of bread baked with *chorizo* and bacon inside: an instant sandwich.

Sweet biscuits, cakes and breakfast pastries are usually purchased rather than baked in the home. Some are sold in the bakery, others in a specialist *pastelería* where assistants require a degree in origami paper folding to achieve the feats of packaging expected. At weekends ladies bear immaculate parcels of goodies home to the family, a Basque custard tart or a *Brazo de Gitano*, a 'gypsy's arm' sponge stuffed with caramel cream. Northerners bake with butter, while the rest of the country use pork fat and olive oil. Little, crumbly biscuits are a speciality of central Spain and the South. The *panadería* in Seville's Triana market is a treasure-trove of these *polvorones* and *roscas*, each individually wrapped in old-fashioned greaseproof paper stamped with a sacred virgin or a company crest.

empanadas
galician flat pies

The fortunate locals of Santiago de Compostela can pick up a slice of ready-made *empanada* from any number of the bakeries around the city. There is a myriad of flavours on offer too, such as scallop, octopus, lamprey, tuna, salt cod or pork. Some have a cornmeal or a pastry crust, but the most popular are encased in a deliciously thin bread dough.

Making an *empanada* is quite a time-consuming business but your labours will be rewarded with a remarkably resilient transportable feast.

serves 8–12 as a snack

for the crust

20 g/³/₄ oz fresh yeast or
  1 tsp dried easy-blend yeast
3 tbsp hand-hot water
350 g/12 oz strong white flour
125 g/4¹/₂ oz cornmeal, *masa
  harina* or finely ground *polenta*
¹/₂ tbsp salt
50 ml/2 fl oz white wine

100 ml/3¹/₂ fl oz olive oil, plus
  extra for oiling
50 g/2 oz lard, chopped into
  1 cm/¹/₂ inch dice, you could use
  vegetable fat instead
1 egg, lightly beaten
1 egg lightly beaten, to seal and
  glaze

Mix the yeast and water to a paste in a small bowl.

Place the flour, cornmeal, salt, wine, olive oil, lard, beaten egg and yeast paste in a large bowl and stir the mixture to combine, then pull it together with your hands. It should feel soft and quite sticky, if there is any dry flour left in the bowl add a splash more water. You will have a job to roll the dough out thinly later if it is too dry.

Knead the dough for a couple of minutes until well combined and smooth. Place it back in the bowl and cover with a baking tray or clingfilm and leave to rise for at least 1 hour, or until it has doubled in size.

Meanwhile, make your filling (see recipes opposite).

Preheat the oven to 200°C/400°F/Gas Mark 6.

On a lightly floured surface, roll out half the dough to a 5 mm/¹/₄ inch thickness to fit a large baking sheet. Oil the baking sheet and lay the dough on top. Now pile on the filling, spreading it evenly and leaving a 2cm/³/₄ inch margin around the edge. Brush the edge with a little beaten egg.

Roll the remaining dough to the same size and lay it over the filling. Crimp the edges together, twisting over the dough to form a rope-like edge. Brush the entire *empanada* with beaten egg and, using a fork, pierce the top with lots of holes.

Leave to rest for 10 minutes, then bake in the hot oven for 20–30 minutes, or until the crust is nicely browned.

relleno de lomo
pork and chorizo filling

100 ml/3½ fl oz olive oil
250 g/9 oz soft cooking *chorizo*
  (see page 49), finely sliced
500 g/1 lb 2 oz pork loin,
  finely diced
4 onions, finely sliced

2 red peppers, finely sliced
2 garlic cloves, crushed
1 tsp sweet smoked paprika
½ tsp dried oregano
2 tbsp tomato purée
salt and freshly ground black pepper

Heat the olive oil in a large pan, add the *chorizo* and fry until the fat begins to render giving the oil a rich, orange glow. Remove the *chorizo* and then add the pork to the pan in 2 batches, allowing it to brown a little. Set the pork aside with the *chorizo*.

Next cook the onions in the same oil until really soft, at least 20 minutes, stirring from time to time. Add the peppers and continue cooking until these soften too. Add the garlic and paprika and then, once you can really smell the garlic, add the oregano and tomato purée.

Stir in the pork and *chorizo* and season with salt and pepper to taste.

relleno de pulpo
octopus stuffing

150 ml/5 fl oz olive oil
4 onions, finely sliced
3 garlic cloves, crushed
1 tsp sweet non-smoked paprika

1 tbsp chopped fresh parsley
1 kg/2¼ lb cooked octopus
  (see page 25), cut into chunks
salt and freshly ground black pepper

Heat the olive oil in a large pan, add the onions and fry slowly until soft and golden. Be patient, the more gently you fry the base, the more delicious the result. Sweet onions are key to a fabulous *cmpanada*.

Add the garlic and stir over a medium heat for a minute or two before sprinkling in the paprika and parsley.

Remove the pan from the heat and stir in the octopus. Season with salt and pepper to taste.

coca de trempó
vegetable coca

Staggering around a market laden with heavy baskets of goodies can be a hungry business and a perfect excuse for a nibble on the move. *Coca* is the Spanish answer to *pizza* – a thin dough topped with delicious vegetables or even a sugary crust, but unlike its Italian cousin very rarely containing cheese. It is sold by the slice from bakeries and market stands all over Catalonia, Valencia and the Balearic Islands. Although it would make a delicious lunch or picnic dish, I have yet to get a piece home. There is something delightfully decadent about scoffing it on the street, straight from the greaseproof paper.

This recipe comes from Mallorca, where I spent many a winter while working as a chef on boats.

serves 6–8 as a snack

for the dough – enough for 1 large
    coca
**1 tbsp fresh yeast or
    1 tsp dried yeast
about 290 ml/scant 10 fl oz warm
    water or enough to make
    the dough
500 g/1 lb 2 oz strong white flour
1 tbsp salt**

**4 tbsp olive oil, plus extra for oiling
2 tbsp white wine**

for the topping
**4 green peppers, de-seeded and
    sliced
4 medium tomatoes, sliced
1 onion, sliced
2 tbsp olive oil
salt**

Place the yeast in a small bowl with a little warm water and stir to give a loose paste.

Place the flour in a large mixing bowl and add the yeast, salt, olive oil, wine and enough water to make a soft, but not too sticky, dough. Knead the dough for about 5 minutes until silky and stretchy, then place it in a lightly oiled bowl and cover with a baking sheet or some clingfilm. Leave to rise for at least an hour at room temperature, or until it has doubled in size.

Preheat the oven to 200°C/400°F/Gas Mark 6.

Oil a large baking sheet.

On a lightly floured surface, roll out the dough into a large rectangle, about 2 cm/3/4 inch thick and lay on the prepared baking sheet.

Place all the topping ingredients in a bowl with the olive oil and salt. Toss the vegetables to cover them with oil and lay them attractively them on top of the dough.

Bake in the oven for 20–25 minutes until the crust is crisp and browned.

Tip *Coca* is usually served at room temperature, making it a fabulous make-ahead treat for a long train journey or a day on the beach.

pan de centeno gallego
galician rye bread

Galicia is home to many fabulous traditional breads. Ironically, these gloriously chewy, dense loaves were born out of poverty. When wheat was too expensive an option the locally grown rye and corn were used instead. Nowadays a few small bakeries in the west still produce the moist *pan de maíz y centeno*, a hefty dough traditionally eaten with sardines. Meanwhile, a mixture of rye and wheat flour produces the characteristic *pan de país*, or country bread found all over the region.

You will need to begin this bread at least 24 hours in advance.

makes 1 large loaf

for the starter
a thumbnail of fresh yeast
100 ml/3½ fl oz water
100 g/4 oz strong white bread flour

for the dough
10 g/⅓ oz fresh yeast
350–400 ml/12–15 fl oz hand-hot water

250 g/9 oz rye flour
250 g/9 oz strong white bread flour, plus extra sifted, for sprinkling
2 tsp salt
olive oil, for oiling

Mix the yeast to a paste with 2 tbsp water in a bowl and then stir in the flour and remaining water. Place in a large bowl with plenty of room for expansion. Cover with a damp cloth and leave at room temperature for at least 24 hours or better still for 2 days. It should smell slightly sour. If you are not ready to use the starter yet, keep it in a jar in the refrigerator.

For the dough, mix the yeast and a couple of spoonfuls of the water to a creamy paste. Place the rye flour and strong flour in a large mixing bowl, make a well in the centre and add the salt, creamed yeast and starter dough. Next add enough of the hand-hot water to make a soft but not too sticky dough. Tip the dough onto a large flat surface and knead for about 10 minutes. It will become smooth but do not expect too much elasticity since rye does not contain the same stretchy gluten as wheat.

Place the dough back in the bowl, cover and leave to rise at room temperature for at least 1 hour, maybe 2 hours, or until it has doubled in size. Oil a large baking sheet.

Knock back the dough and shape it into a large, flat round. Place the dough on the prepared baking sheet, cover with a damp tea towel and leave to rise again until doubled in size.

Preheat the oven to 200°C/400°F/Gas Mark 6.

Sprinkle the dough with sifted flour. Bake for 1 hour, or until the bread just slips off the baking sheet and sounds hollow when tapped underneath. Leave to cool on a wire rack.

Variations
You may like to vary the proportion of rye to wheat flour. More rye and the bread will be denser and heavier, more wheat and it will produce an altogether lighter crumb.

Sultanas can be added to the dough after it has been knocked back. I find it easiest to incorporate the fruit by flattening the dough as if making a pizza, sprinkling with sultanas and then rolling up tightly. At this point you can shape the dough as above.

carquinyolis
almond biscuits

Bakeries all over Catalonia sell bags of these tasty little biscuits. Beware, they are hard enough to chip a tooth on, but soft and heavenly once dipped in a *café solo*, or espresso, or a sweet sherry, which they soak up like a sponge. *Carquinyolis* are closely related to Italian *cantuccini*, although to doubt their local origin would be heresy in these parts.

These biscuits are traditionally made with almonds, the national nut, but you could try them with hazelnuts instead, in which case I would replace the lemon zest with orange.

makes about 30 biscuits

olive oil, for oiling
75 g/3 oz whole blanched almonds
125 g/4½ oz plain flour
½ tsp baking powder
75 g/3 oz caster sugar

1 egg, beaten
1 tsp grated lemon zest
1 tsp vanilla extract or a good
** pinch of ground cinnamon**

Preheat the oven to 180°C/350°F/Gas Mark 4.

Oil a large baking sheet.

Toast the almonds in the oven for 5–10 minutes, or until just beginning to colour.

Sift the flour and baking powder together into a large bowl and make a well in the centre. Add the rest of the ingredients and mix together, first with a spoon and then with your hands, a thoroughly sticky job.

On a lightly floured surface, roll the mixture into 3 long logs and place on the prepared baking sheet, leaving a little space between them for expansion while cooking. Bake in the oven for about 15 minutes, or until the dough begins to brown. Remove from the oven and cut the dough on the diagonal, into 2 cm/³/4 inch thick slices.

Place the slices, cut-side down, on the baking sheet and bake for a further 5–10 minutes until golden. Leave to cool on a wire rack.

Tips *Carquinyolis* make wonderful presents if you can purchase small cellophane bags or pretty little tins to store them in. They will keep for weeks in an airtight container.

Try these little biscuits with the poached peaches or pears on page 169. They will soak up all the wonderful cooking juices.

magdalenas
breakfast sponge cakes

These little cakes are a Spanish institution and the perfect accompaniment to a hot chocolate or coffee. *Churros*, or dough fritters, may have hit the international stage as the most popular breakfast snack but they are rarely eaten at home. They are best bought from the market van or café, hot and crisp, straight from the sizzling cauldrons of oil. Meanwhile, *magdalenas* grace the domestic table all over the country.

There are regional variations: the butter-rich *sobao pasiego* from the dairy lands of the North, the interior's pork fat *mantecado* and the denser-textured olive oil *magdalena* from the South.

You will require 16 paper fairy cake cases.

Tips when baking

Whenever you are baking cakes or soufflés use the bottom heat option on your oven, if you have the choice. As the heat rises it will help the mixture rise too.

Try not to open the oven door to peep at your cakes for at least half of their cooking time or the sudden drop in temperature could cause the cakes to sink.

makes 16

3 medium eggs
250 g/9 oz caster sugar
250 g/9 oz natural yogurt
grated zest of 1 lemon

5 tbsp olive oil
250 g/9 oz self-raising flour, or
  250 g/9 oz plain flour and
  4 tsp baking powder

Preheat the oven to 180°C/350°F/Gas Mark 4.

Beat the eggs and sugar together with a whisk in a large bowl until they become pale and mousse-like. Whisk in the yogurt, lemon zest and olive oil.

Sift the flour, with the baking powder if using, into a bowl, then make a well in the centre and add the egg mixture. Stir until evenly combined.

Divide the mixture carefully between 16 paper cases, filling to about two-thirds full and bake in the oven for 20–25 minutes, or until risen and golden.

Leave the cakes to cool on a wire rack and store in an airtight tin if you are not eating them straight away.

brazo de gitano
sponge roulade (gypsy's arm)

Quite how this popular sponge roulade earned its rather bizarre name is a mystery but it is sold in *pastelerías* all over the country, invariably filled with a deliciously creamy custard. I came across a similar recipe from León with the elevated title of Tronco del Vaticano, or Vatican Log, this time covered with delicious chocolate and filled with strawberries. Another version, from Tenerife in The Canary Islands, was filled with *dulce de leche*, a thick caramelized milk from South America, and slices of local banana. So, although you may feel a little intimidated by all the whisking, folding and rolling, once mastered this is an extremely versatile recipe.

serves 8

for the sponge
melted butter or olive oil, for greasing or oiling
100 g/4 oz plain flour, plus ½ tbsp extra for dusting
5 eggs, separated
100 g/4 oz caster sugar, plus extra for dusting
grated zest of 1 lemon
2 tbsp icing sugar, for dusting

for the traditional *crema pastelera* filling
250 ml/8 fl oz full fat milk
½ stick cinnamon
pared zest of ½ lemon
3 egg yolks
2 tbsp caster sugar
1 tbsp cornflour
1 tsp vanilla extract, or a little rum, brandy or sherry

Preheat the oven to 220°C/425°F/Gas Mark 7.

Line a 25 x 38 cm/10 x15 inch tin with baking paper and brush with the melted butter or olive oil, then dust with the ½ tbsp flour.

Beat the egg yolks with half of the sugar and the lemon zest until really pale and thick. You will need an electric whisk for this or biceps like Popeye. The process will be speeded up if you place the bowl over a pan of very hot water.

Sift the flour into the mixture, carefully folding at the same time.

Next whisk the whites in a separate clean bowl until stiff peaks form, then add the remaining sugar and whisk again to a glossy meringue. Fold the meringue carefully but thoroughly into the yolk mixture.

Gently pour or spoon the mixture into the prepared tin and carefully smooth the surface. Bake in the oven for about 10 minutes until the sponge is springy and golden.

Meanwhile, prepare a sheet of baking paper, a little larger than your tin and sprinkle it with a little sugar. Invert your cooked sponge onto the paper and carefully peel away the lining paper. Trim away any crusty edges.

While the sponge is still warm, roll it up loosely from the long edge, and leave to cool.

Now you can make the filling. Heat the milk, cinnamon and lemon zest gently in a small saucepan and leave to infuse for at least 10 minutes.

Meanwhile, beat the eggs and sugar together in a large bowl, then add the cornflour, stirring to remove any lumps. Strain the milk, a little at a time onto the egg mixture, stirring as you go.

Rinse out the pan and pour in the egg and milk mixture. Stir over a medium heat for about 5–10 minutes until the custard bubbles and thickens. Add the vanilla extract, or a little rum, brandy or sherry, if you prefer and leave to cool.

Unroll the sponge carefully, just enough to fill it and spread over the *crema pastelera*. Roll the cake up again, using the paper to help you, and dust with icing sugar.

For the Chocolate and Strawberry Vatican Log

Slice about 250 g/9 oz of strawberries (raspberries are delicious too), and lay them on top of the custard filling before rolling up the sponge.

Carefully melt 300 g/10 oz of good quality plain dark chocolate with 50 g/2 oz unsalted butter. The most foolproof way is in a bowl set over a pan of simmering water, but you may just dare to use your microwave, on its lowest setting for about a minute.

Leave the mixture to cool and thicken for a minute or two before pouring over the roulade.

And, for those with a very sweet tooth...

The Tenerife Banana Roulade

Make a half quantity of *crema pastelera* and mix this with 5 tbsp *dulce de leche*, a thick caramelized milk from South America now available in Spain and elsewhere too. Slice 5 tiny Canary Island bananas, or 3 ripe bananas and place in a bowl. Squeeze over the juice of 1 lemon.

Spread the *crema* mixture over the sponge, top with the bananas and roll up as before.

vegetables

You can't fail to be impressed by the huge mounds of vegetables in a Spanish market. The climate is perfect for growing peppers, tomatoes and aubergines – that sunshine trio associated with summer days and long Mediterranean lunches. The hothouse varieties can never begin to compare with the flavour of naturally ripened produce. And yet, many tourists are at a loss as to where all those glorious fresh vegetables end up; not in the *tapas* bars or restaurants it would seem.

Vegetables are relatively cheap, usually simple to prepare and play a background role in the professional kitchen. Who would go out and pay for a chef to grill a few peppers when you could prepare them just as well at home? Yet a vegetable *sofrito* of onions, tomato and garlic is the starting point of many of the popular fish and meat stews enjoyed in restaurants all over the country. The fact is that

vegetables are not seen as accompaniments, the notion of "meat and two veg" is just non-existent. They are used in sauces or served as a dish apart, often pepped up with a touch of cured pork. Of course there are a few aristocrats on the vegetable patch that break all the rules, commanding high prices and being savoured as a delicacies in their own right. Amongst these are the *Piquillo* pepper of Lodosa, the artichoke from Tudela and, perhaps the most eagerly awaited, Vall's delectable *calçot* that resembles an oversized spring onion. Back at home vegetables are an everyday staple. Many meals begin with a salad, soup, or plate of simple boiled or grilled vegetables.

Climate and terrain vary massively across the country and consequently, so does the produce on offer. Turnip tops, cabbages, chard and potatoes are not the first vegetables that spring to mind at the mention of Spain. Yet in damp Galicia these are the

140

mainstays of all the traditional soups and stews. Head east to the sun-drenched Ebro Valley of Rioja and Navarre and you find artichokes, cardoons, asparagus and peppers. Here cultivation is only possible with the vast scale of irrigation, much of it dating back to the time of the Moors. The Basques and the Catalans are wild mushroom fanatics, and collectors will often turn up at local markets with a basket of woodland jewels. If you are an enthusiast too then you should look up Petràs at his stall in the depths of Barcelona's Boqueria with an extraordinary range of mushrooms both fresh and dried. Valencia is known for its oranges and rice but a surprising discovery is the local infatuation with green beans. Entire stalls are devoted to countless varieties of French beans, broad beans, butter beans and peas. Ladies are industriously podding between customers so that the lazier ones among us can buy beans by the bag, ready for the pot

or *paella*. Meanwhile, down south, long summers see avocados sitting alongside autumnal pumpkins and sweet potatoes.

Fresh, ripe vegetables straight from the *huerta*, vegetable plot, are always the best. Tomatoes, fully ripened on the vine, that have never seen a refrigerator or a glut of courgettes, brought straight to market. There is often a huddle of small-scale producers with their baskets and buckets of home-grown potatoes, garlic, peppers, or whatever the season brings. In springtime Gerona there are bunches of the spindly wild asparagus collected from hedgerows while strings of deep red onions are the highlight at an October market in Potes. These are the surprises that give markets their magic. Menus miraculously evolve as you become increasingly laden with all the unexpected treats that weren't on the shopping list.

alcachofas en escabeche
artichokes with wine and vinegar

This edible thistle flower is yet another crop that was popularized by the Moors. Today the tender, oval Blanca de Tudela is the most highly esteemed variety but the larger, spherical Alcachofa de Valencia has a wonderful flavour too. Artichokes are available from October through to late spring, becoming more economical as the season progresses, worth keeping in mind when you consider that only about a quarter of their weight is edible.

serves 4 as a starter

1 kg/2¼ lb artichokes
2 lemons, 1 halved and 1 juiced
4 tbsp olive oil
8 garlic cloves, thinly sliced
2 tbsp plain flour
100 ml/3½ fl oz white wine

1 bay leaf
1 sprig of fresh thyme
10 whole black peppercorns
salt
2 tbsp sherry vinegar

Prepare the artichokes (see right), cutting them in half or quarters depending on their size, and place in a bowl of acidulated water.

Heat the olive oil in a large frying pan, add the garlic and fry over a medium heat until just golden. Do not burn it or the entire dish will be bitter. Remove the garlic with a slotted spoon, every last slither, and set aside in a large saucepan.

Next remove the artichokes from the acidulated water a few at a time, dry off with some kitchen paper and fry in the garlic infused oil. Do not crowd the pan or they will not caramelize. Once beautifully browned, place the artichokes with the garlic.

Add the flour to the frying pan and stir over the heat for a couple of minutes. Pour in the wine, stirring to prevent any lumps from forming. You may need to add a little water too if the mixture becomes too thick.

Pour the wine sauce over the artichokes together with the bay leaf, thyme, peppercorns, a pinch of salt and enough water to cover them and simmer for 20 minutes. Add the sherry vinegar and simmer for a further 5–10 minutes, or until the artichokes are meltingly tender. If the sauce seems extremely thin you may like to remove the artichokes and reduce it over a high heat for a moment or two.

Serve hot or at room temperature.

Tip   Toasted pine kernels or fried strips of *jamón Serrano* would make a delicious garnish.

Buying artichokes
The Spanish pick their artichokes deliciously young and tender. The size will depend on the variety but look for tightly closed, shiny leaves.

To prepare artichoke halves or quarters
Half-fill a large pan with water and add the juice of 1 lemon, you will need to submerge the cleaned artichokes as you prepare them to stop them oxidizing and turning black.

Next trim the stalks and peel off the rough outer skin, then remove the tough outer leaves. Chop across the remaining leaves, about a third of the way down, you should now be able to delve into the centre with a teaspoon and scrape out the hairy choke. Halve or quarter the artichokes, rubbing any cut surfaces with a halved lemon and then placing in the acidulated water.

Whole artichokes may be soaked upside down in salty water for an hour, in order to remove any insects, before being roasted or placed on the barbecue. Once the base is tender – test with a knife or skewer – they are ready to be enjoyed with some extra virgin olive oil. Remove a leaf at a time, dipping its succulent base in the oil, until you reach the centre. Discard the hairy choke and savour the heart.

crema de pimientos
red pepper soup

The subtle spicing and sweetness of this soup is typical of much southern Spanish cooking, reflecting it's Moorish heritage. The recipe comes from Granada, a city crowned by the palace of the last Nasrid sultans: the legendary Alhambra. Watching the sunset cast its fuchsia glow over the fortress walls is spectacular. Rhythmic clapping and wails of Flamenco resound around the narrow alleys of the Medieval quarter and modern Spain seems a world away.

serves 4

3 tbsp olive oil
5 red peppers, roasted and peeled (see page 144)
3 onions, diced
2 garlic cloves, crushed
½ tsp ground cumin
½ tsp sweet paprika

1 tsp *miel de caña* (see note on page 156) or dark muscovado sugar
850 ml/1½ pints home-made chicken stock
salt
juice of ½–1 lemon to taste
4 tbsp single cream

Heat the olive oil in a large saucepan, add the peppers, onions and garlic and fry gently until the onions become soft and translucent.

Sprinkle with the spices together with the *miel de caña*, or sugar, and stir over the heat for 1 minute.

Next add the chicken stock, the real thing please, a stock cube will leave the soup tasting thin and salty, and simmer for 10 minutes.

Transfer the soup to a blender and process until smooth, then strain, if you like and season with salt and lemon juice to taste.

Reheat the soup with the cream just before serving. Take care not to let it boil or your cream will split. If you are a scatty cook, and I speak from experience, then perhaps a dollop of double cream is a safer option – you can boil it to death with no ill effect.

Buying peppers

Peppers should be firm and shiny with no sign of a wrinkle. Green peppers have a sharper, fresher flavour than their red counterparts and can sometimes cause indigestion when eaten raw. Hardly a surprise when you consider they are unripe red or yellow peppers.

Red peppers are delicious raw or roasted. I find even the less exciting hothouse varieties can be transformed to deliciously rich and creamy success stories when roasted. But there is no doubt that nothing can beat their deep red, sun-ripened cousins.

ensalada de pimientos con naranja
red pepper and orange salad

This is a truly sunny salad from Andalucia, which is best eaten in late autumn with the new season oranges and the last of the sun-ripened peppers. The dish bursts with colour and zippy flavour, making a glorious accompaniment to simply grilled fish.

serves 4

6 red peppers, roasted, peeled and sliced into ribbons
1/2 sweet onion, halved and finely sliced
2 oranges, peeled, halved and sliced
2 tomatoes, halved and sliced
100 g/4 oz green, marinated olives

1 tsp cumin seeds, roasted (see page 108)
2 garlic cloves, roughly chopped
1/2 tsp salt
4 tbsp extra virgin olive oil
lemon juice or vinegar, to taste (optional)
a few fresh coriander leaves (optional)

Place the sliced pepper, onion, orange and tomatoes in a bowl with the olives.

Next you can make the aromatic dressing. Crush the cumin seeds in a mortar with a pestle, then add the garlic and salt. Pound to a paste before adding the extra virgin olive oil, drop by drop as you stir, creating a creamy emulsion.

You may need to add a little lemon juice or vinegar if the oranges are particularly sweet.

Toss the salad in the dressing and leave to macerate for about an hour. You could add a few fresh coriander leaves too.

Variation   Substitute 1 small can *atún blanco* (white albacore tuna, see page 39), drained, for the oranges and proceed as above. Garnish with parsley in place of the coriander.

Roasting peppers
Roasting rather than grilling a pepper to remove its skin brings out its natural sweetness. The slower the roast the more fabulous the flavour, no oven temperatures or timings required! The only rule of thumb is that the skin should look bubbly and blistered. Once cooked leave the peppers to cool – I tend to cover them with an upturned bowl, the steam seems to help the skins slip off. Slip off the skins over the bowl – not under cold running water – it would be sacrilege to wash away those delicious juices. Strain off the juices and reserve; they are ideal for adding to a salad dressing or soup. Keep the cooked peeled peppers for a few days in the refrigerator covered in olive oil.

fritá de calabaza
fried pumpkin with peppers and almonds

Pumpkin is immensely popular in Southern Spain and very conveniently it can be purchased by the slice in most local markets. The subtle, creamy flesh is used in many vegetable stews while sweet and fibrous winter varieties are cooked with sugar to produce *cabello de angel*, angel hair, a delicious filling for pastries and pies such as the famous *pastel de Córdoba*.

serves 4

4 tbsp olive oil
500 g/1 lb 2 oz floury potatoes, peeled and thinly sliced
500 g/1 lb 2 oz pumpkin, peeled and finely sliced
1 green pepper, de-seeded and sliced
a pinch of salt

for the *picadillo*

2 tbsp olive oil
5 garlic cloves, peeled
2 slices of yesterday's white bread
1–2 tsp cumin seeds, roasted (see page 108)
a pinch of salt
10 almonds, roasted (see page 108)

Begin by starting the *picadillo*. Heat the 2 tbsp olive oil in a large pan, add the garlic and fry until golden, then remove from the pan and set aside.

Next, using the same oil, fry the bread until golden then set it aside too.

Add the 4 tbsp olive oil to the pan and fry the potatoes over a low heat for about 10 minutes. Add the pumpkin and the green pepper and stir to coat in a little oil. Sprinkle with a pinch of salt and continue to fry until the pumpkin and green pepper begin to soften, about 10 minutes.

Meanwhile, you can make the *picadillo*. Using a mortar and pestle, crush the cumin seeds, then add the golden garlic with a little salt and crush, followed by the almonds and lastly the fried bread. You could, of course, whiz everything in a small food processor or blender with a tablespoon of water.

Stir the *picadillo* into the pumpkin mixture and serve.

Tip You could garnish the vegetables with some finely chopped parsley, mint or coriander.

Buying and storing pumpkin
A whole pumpkin, free of cracks or soft spots will keep for months in an airy place. Look for specimens that are heavy for their size.

It is extremely convenient to buy pumpkin by the slice, escaping the perilous task of hacking through the tough skin and also avoiding mountains of leftovers. But, once cut the flesh will lose flavour and nutritional value in a trice so use within a day of purchase. If you must keep it for any longer make sure to remove the seeds and fibrous centre, as these will go off quickly.

ajo blanco
chilled garlic and almond soup

Those strings of garlic that sing of Mediterranean markets, are more likely to be snapped up by the tourist than the passionate cook. Years ago when each family had their own vegetable patch plaiting the garlic was the ideal way of drying and preserving the bulbs for winter. They were stored in a cool outhouse, cellar or larder until needed. Today these decorative plaits find their way into the hot, steamy kitchen of the modern home where the garlic turns stale and rancid in a trice. So, unless you are warding off vampires or feeding the five thousand, best buy your garlic one bulb at a time.

The fresh, young bulbs of summer garlic, sometimes known as wet garlic, are ideal for this recipe. The cloves are sweet, mild and less likely to cause indigestion than the more pungent dried variety.

Buying and storing garlic
Purchase garlic in small quantities, the sooner you use it the better. The flavour becomes increasingly acrid and pungent as the garlic ages.

Should your garlic begin to sprout it is no longer fit for the pot. You could always plant the cloves and then harvest their chive-like shoots. These *ajetes* are often thrown into a *revuelto*, scrambled egg.

serves 6

2 slices of stale white bread, crusts removed
100 g/4 oz blanched almonds
2 garlic cloves, roughly chopped
1.2 litres/2 pints chilled water
3 tbsp extra virgin olive oil

1–2 tbsp white wine vinegar
salt
18 sweet white grapes or 9 tiger prawns, cooked, peeled and halved lengthways, to garnish

Process the bread, almonds, garlic and half the water in a blender or food processor until smooth.

Next, with the motor still running, drizzle in the extra virgin olive oil. Add a little vinegar, a pinch of salt and enough water to give a milky consistency. Taste and adjust the seasoning, adding more vinegar or salt if necessary.

Serve garnished with the grapes, which are traditionally peeled – true dedication – not a quality I possess, or three prawn halves per serving. The garnish should be sweet to counter balance the bite of the garlic.

ajotomate
tomato and garlic salad

Sunlight streams through stained-glass windows onto the mountains of luscious produce in Valencia's Art Deco style market place. The *huerta* or vegetable garden of Valencia is famed throughout Spain. The fertile plains have been intensively cultivated since medieval times using irrigation channels designed by the Moors. Should the quantity of raw garlic seem a little daunting, then try blanching the cloves first (see the tip on the right) to mellow their flavour.

serves 4

2–4 garlic cloves, roughly chopped
salt
1 large, very ripe tomato, peeled and diced
150 ml/5 fl oz extra virgin olive oil
1 tbsp red wine vinegar
sugar (optional)

4–6 tomatoes of varying ripeness and size, sliced, try using a couple of green streaked Raf, salad tomatoes, to add texture and flavour
1 tsp toasted cumin seeds (see page 108)

Using a mortar and pestle, grind the garlic and a large pinch of salt into a creamy paste.

Add the diced tomato and continue to work the mixture until it is smooth.

Next, pour in the extra virgin olive oil and vinegar, stirring all the time. Taste and add more salt if necessary. You may even like to add a pinch of sugar.

Arrange your sliced tomatoes on a serving platter and tip over the dressing. Sprinkle with cumin seeds and leave to stand for at least 15 minutes to allow the flavours to develop before serving at room temperature.

Tip This dressing also works fantastically well with fresh French beans.

Preparing garlic
The more finely you chop garlic the more the pungent compounds are released and thus the more intensely flavoured your dish will be.

Garlic crushed in the mortar or under the flat blade of a knife gives the most potent results. Slices of garlic are a gentler option while, for a more subtle flavour altogether, cook with whole cloves and remove them before serving.

Blanching whole garlic cloves in boiling in water for 2–3 minutes is a useful way of reducing the potency of garlic before crushing in sauces or dressings. Roasting the cloves or even the entire bulbs of garlic until meltingly soft and creamy also gives a deliciously mellow result (see Aubergine Caviar on page 156).

gazpacho

High summer in Southern Spain is a stifling affair, rubber soles become tacky on red-hot paving stones and even the shady narrow streets offer little respite from the oppressive heat. On days such as these there is nothing more appetizing than a deliciously chilled bowl of fresh gazpacho.

After an hour pottering around the weekly market in Trujillo, Estramadura, I virtually crawled into a restaurant to escape the asphyxiating midday sun. The gazpacho was glorious, cooled with a rather unorthodox basil ice cube. You could try it; just throw finely chopped basil into the ice-cube tray, cover with water and freeze.

The tomatoes must be very ripe for this recipe: bursting with sun and flavour; the mass-produced cotton wool variety just won't do.

serves 6–8

3 slices of white, country bread
900 g/2 lb tomatoes, peeled,
  de-seeded and chopped
1 medium cucumber, peeled and
  roughly chopped
3 red peppers, de-seeded and
  roughly chopped
2 garlic cloves, roughly chopped
2 spring onions, sliced (optional)
100 ml/3½ fl oz extra virgin olive oil
salt
1–2 tbsp sherry vinegar to taste

to garnish – any of the following
2 eggs, hard-boiled and finely
  diced
slices of spring onion
cucumber, very finely diced
red pepper, very finely
  diced
tiny croûtons, fried in olive oil
tiny cubes of *jamón Serrano*

Place the bread in a small bowl and cover with water. Leave to soak.

Next put all the vegetables in a food processor or blender and process well.

Add the soaked bread to the vegetables together with the extra virgin olive oil and process, adding just enough water to get a soupy consistency. Remember that if you add ice cubes when you serve the gazpacho you will dilute it further. Season with the salt and vinegar to taste.

If you are a true perfectionist you may like to strain the soup, but I am just too impatient.

Serve well chilled with a few ice cubes and a selection of the garnishes above. The garnishes are traditionally served from tiny bowls or ramekins for guests to help themselves, but for a more contemporary twist, you could arrange them attractively in the bowls and pour the soup from a jug at the table.

Peeling and de-seeding tomatoes
Score a small cross through the skin at the base of each tomato. Place them in a bowl and cover with boiling water. Leave for about 10 seconds for very ripe tomatoes and more like 20 for a harder salad tomato. Drain the tomatoes, cool under the cold running water and strip off the skin using your cross as an easy starting point.

De-seeding tomatoes is only really necessary if you are making a raw sauce or soup where they might affect the texture; the seeds tend to break down during cooking. If you are straining your recipe you will remove the seeds in any case.

mermelada de tomàquet
tomato jam

Catalan tomato jam is an ideal way of using up a glut of slightly overripe tomatoes. Try it with toast for breakfast or as an accompaniment to goat's cheese.

makes 2 jars

1 kg/2¼ lb ripe tomatoes
caster sugar (see below)

juice of, and 1 strip of zest from, 1 unwaxed lemon

Peel the tomatoes by scalding them in a bowl of boiling water for about a minute. Tip away the water and the skins should slip off the flesh easily.

Remove the seeds from the tomatoes and chop finely. Now weigh the tomato flesh and weigh out an equal quantity of sugar.

Place all the ingredients in a large saucepan with plenty of room for the mixture to boil without spilling. Bring to a rolling boil, but be careful it will erupt like a volcano, and let it bubble away, uncovered for about 10 minutes. Reduce the heat and simmer, stirring once in a while, for about 40 minutes.

To test whether your jam is ready place a spoonful on a cold saucer, preferably chilled from the refrigerator. Leave the jam for 1 minute and then slowly tip the saucer, if the jam has begun to set and formed a skin it is ready. If not, then keep simmering until it does. In any case this jam will be a little runnier than most.

Pour into sterilized 450 g/1 lb jars (see right) and cover with lids or greaseproof paper.

Storing tomatoes
Tomatoes become tasteless when refrigerated so keep them in the fruit bowl where they will continue to ripen and gain in flavour.

Should your tomatoes become a little overripe and soft you could squeeze them over country bread as alternative to butter. Just add a little olive oil and salt and hey presto you have the Catalan classic *pa amb tomàquet,* tomato bread.

Grating tomatoes
Should you require a sizeable quantity of fresh tomato flesh for the Catalan tomato bread, or any casserole or sauce, then grating is the way to go. Just cut the tomato in half around its equator and use a traditional cheese grater. The skin miraculously remains intact, protecting your fingers, whilst the flesh is reduced to a pulp.

To sterilize jars
Wash the jars thoroughly then place in a deep pan and cover with boiling water. Boil for 10 minutes and then drain, upside down on clean kitchen paper.

pisto
simple vegetable stew

This is an infinitely useful Mediterranean vegetable mixture that makes a wonderful snack with some good bread, a great side dish with simply grilled meats and fish, or even a sauce.

serves 4

3 tbsp olive oil
2 onions, sliced
2 red peppers, sliced
2 garlic cloves, crushed
3 courgettes, sliced
200 g/7 oz canned tomatoes or 4 fresh tomatoes, peeled and grated
salt and freshly ground black pepper

Heat the olive oil in a pan, add the onions and peppers and fry until soft. Add the garlic and cook until your kitchen is filled with its scent.

Stir in the courgettes and tomatoes, season with salt and pepper and simmer until tender.

Tip   You may like to add herbs such as thyme, parsley, basil or oregano.

papas arrugadas
wrinkled potatoes

A tropical storm had hit Tenerife. The bus veered dangerously along the road, palms were bent double and tourists had resorted to dancing the Conga around the hotel bar. La Laguna's market had been plunged into darkness in the ensuing power cut, but a few resolute stallholders continued trading. So, I had my first lesson in potato appreciation in the shadows. There were countless classes such as the Red Colorada, the romantically named *ojo de perdiz*, the Partridge Eye, but the king of the castle was undoubtedly the *papa negra oro*: a black potato grown in the island's volcanic soil with famously creamy golden flesh. The most expensive potato in the world! You'll probably have to make do with a more common variety.

serves 4–6

3 tbsp sea salt, plus a large pinch to finish

24 small waxy new potatoes, cleaned well but skins left on, red salad potatoes work well

Place the salt in a saucepan and add enough water to a depth of about 5 cm/2 inches. It's a good idea to use an old pan, as the salt and steam treatment does not do your cookware any favours.

Add the potatoes and cover them with a piece of damp greaseproof paper or a tea towel, then the saucepan lid. Boil for about 20 minutes until the potatoes are tender when skewered.

Next drain the potatoes and return to the pan along with a large pinch of salt. Place the pan over a low heat, shaking and tossing the potatoes until they are dry and wrinkled.

Serve hot or at room temperature with the Hot Red Pepper Sauce on page 104 or as an accompaniment to the Rabbit in Salmorejo Sauce on page 84.

patatas a lo pobre
poorman's potatoes

Life was hard among the picturesque white villages of the Andalucian Alpujarras, before the recent influx of tourists and expats. Their relative isolation, along with the extreme climate of the Sierra Nevada, led to a hearty diet based around a few readily available ingredients. This simple and satisfying potato dish is comfort food at its best, particularly when served with a fried egg and the local cured *jamón Serrano.*

serves 4

6 tbsp olive oil

900 g/2 lb potatoes, use a multi-purpose variety, peeled and finely sliced

1 onion, finely sliced

1 green pepper, finely sliced

1/2 tsp salt

1 garlic clove, crushed

1 tbsp wine vinegar

2 tbsp chopped fresh parsley

Spoon in half of the olive oil into a large frying pan with a well-fitting lid. Next arrange the potatoes, onion and green pepper in layers, seasoning with salt between the layers.

Add the rest of the olive oil, cover with the lid and cook over a very gentle heat for 20–30 minutes until the potatoes are cooked through. Stir from time to time, turning the potatoes over in the oil, it really does not matter if the potatoes break up a little.

Remove the lid and add the garlic, then increase the heat to brown the potatoes slightly. Sprinkle with wine vinegar and parsley before serving.

Tip   You could add 1/2 tsp sweet or spicy paprika at the same time as the garlic or a few cumin seeds will give the Moorish touch.

ensalada de aguacate con huevo de cordoniz
avocado and quail's egg salad

The microclimate around Motril, on the Mediterranean coast, to the South of Granada is subtropical. This was once Europe's great sugar cane plantation but today roadside stalls sell mangoes, papayas and, another relative newcomer, the avocado instead. There were baskets of the tiny, egg-sized local variety at the nearby market in Órgiva, Spain's hippy haven. Plentiful organic produce and some wonderfully hearty home-baked bread were other rare rewards to be found in this land of tepees and tie-dye.

serves 4

6 quail's eggs
2 red peppers, grilled, peeled and de-seeded
3 oranges, peeled
2–4 ripe avocados, depending on their size
150 g/5 oz baby spinach leaves, washed and dried
for the dressing
1 tbsp sherry vinegar
3 tbsp extra virgin olive oil
salt and freshly ground black pepper
to garnish
12 fresh mint leaves
3 tbsp almonds, roasted (see page 108)
½ tsp cumin seeds, toasted (see page 108)

Cook the quail's eggs in a saucepan of boiling water for just over 2 minutes, then plunge them into a bowl of cold water. The yolks should remain an appetizing creamy yellow. Remove the shells and cut the eggs in half.

Slice the peppers into thin ribbons, cut 2 oranges into segments or slices and squeeze the remaining orange, setting the juice aside.

Halve the avocados and remove the stone and skin (see right). Cut the avocado into cubes, place it in a bowl and pour over the orange juice immediately.

Mix all the ingredients for the dressing together in a bowl.

Just prior to serving toss the spinach in the dressing and place on a platter or individual plates. Now arrange the quail's eggs, pepper strips, orange segments and avocado on top, if you toss them all together the eggs and avocado tend to break up and look unattractive.

Sprinkle with the mint leaves, almonds and cumin seeds.

Selecting and storing avocados
Most of the avocados grown in Southern Spain are of the Hass variety with their characteristic bubbly black skin. Many of them are unusually small, barely bigger than a hen's egg, but size is certainly not everything. I have never come across such consistently creamy and delicious avocados in my life.

Touch is the only way to gauge ripeness; the flesh should give a little when pressed gently. If the fruit is rock hard and incidentally much easier to get home safely, then a few days in a warm kitchen will soon ripen it up. If you are in a hurry, with a particular event in mind, 24 hours in a paper bag with a ripe banana should do the trick.

Preparing avocados
Left to its own devices the flesh will oxidize and turn brown almost instantly once cut and, although this will not affect the flavour, it certainly doesn't look very appetizing. Having some lemon, lime or orange juice at the ready and pouring it over the avocado will stop it from discolouring and tastes good too.

fruit

The balmy perfume of ripe peaches on a hot summer's day is hard to beat, although the citrus scent of Christmas must come a very close second. Seasonal ripe fruit, picked in its prime and brought straight to market creates a feast of smells, colours, textures and taste. It is small wonder that Spanish home cooks are not generally known for their desserts. Who would bother when the year is punctuated by the arrival of so many different varieties of fruit? The flavour of a lusciously ripe fig oozing with sticky juices or the exotic sweetness of a tiny Tenerife banana requires no assistance at all.

A January market stall in Ibiza resembles fruit stands all over Mediterranean and Southern Spain, a citrus sea of oranges, clementines, mandarins and lemons. Strangely the Spanish have not adopted our love of marmalade and many of the bitter Seville oranges are left to rot on the trees. Oranges are sometimes used in savoury dishes with fish, duck or pork or whisked into a fabulous *Allioli* (see page 114), but most are squeezed for juice; a popular dessert in restaurants and the healthy choice if you choose not to stir in the accompanying sachet of sugar.

Strawberries come with the spring. Huge *fresónes* from Huelva in the Southwest arrive first, but the smaller *fresas* are always worth waiting for. Pricey punnets of the exquisitely perfumed *fresas de bosque*, or wild strawberries, are sometimes available too, a truly extravagant treat.

The first stone fruits of summer are from the East coast. Refreshing, sweet *nísperas*, Japanese medlars or loquats, used to be greeted with glee when the local citrus season had come to a close and the apricots, cherries and early figs, *brevas*, were yet to arrive. Shopping today, it is more difficult to notice the seasons since much of the fruit is imported or

produced in the monstrous greenhouses of Almeria in the South. But, visit the local market and this month's crop will always be the most economical and delicious.

Thirst-quenching watermelons make their timely appearance in the full heat of summer. Entire vans are stacked from floor to ceiling making a melon avalanche a dangerous possibility should you select the wrong one. Gluts of June cherries make way for luscious nectarines, peaches and my favourites, the flat *paraguayos*, or Saturn peaches, somewhat unglamorously re-christened doughnut peaches by one British retailer! The white-fleshed fruit is consistently sweet and a recipe for a sticky chin, since you just have to try one there and then.

Plums, apples and pears are most suited to Spain's cooler Northern half. One bite of a golden greengage in Santiago de Compostela brought back childhood memories of orchard fruit picking. It was heaven, incomparable with the insipid flesh of an imported plum. Meanwhile, pears from Rioja, a very tasty prospect poached in the local wine, and *Reineta*, or Russet apples, from León travel well and are celebrated all over the country. Autumnal quinces fill kitchens with steam as laborious housewives busy themselves making the slabs of firm quince paste, *Dulce de Membrillo* (see page 170) that make such a popular accompaniment to cheese. The sloes of the Basque country and Navarre have a more masculine fan base. They are a vital ingredient in Pacharán: a digestif made with *anis*, an aniseed liqueur, coffee beans, cinnamon sticks and whatever else the family recipe dictates.

The subtropical climes of the Canary Islands, and a small corner of southern Andalucia put a few exotic fruits on the menu too. Mangoes, custard apples, the odd pineapple and, of course, the ambrosial dwarf bananas.

naranjas caramelizadas
caramelized oranges

I was after half a dozen oranges at the market in Órgiva and was glad to find an old chap with a wheelbarrow load for sale. Unfortunately he was so intent on selling the lot that you could only buy them by the bucketful. The fruit was such a bargain that I even offered the same price for half the quantity but he was having none of it. So eventually, laden like a packhorse, I got home to make this timeless dessert, thankful for his resolve.

serves 4

4 unwaxed oranges
4 tbsp Grand Marnier or sweet
  Pedro Jimenez sherry

3 tbsp white granulated sugar
3 tbsp water

Remove the zest from the oranges and set aside.

Peel the oranges, removing all the bitter white pith, then cut the oranges into slices and remove any seeds. Put the oranges into a serving dish and pour over the alcohol.

Now you can make the caramel. Place the sugar and water in a small saucepan and cook gently over a low heat until the sugar has dissolved. Increase the heat and allow the sugar to begin to caramelize, turning light golden brown, but do not stir. Remove the pan from the heat; the caramel will carry on cooking. You are aiming for a light brick brown colour. Add the orange zest and pour over the oranges.

Leave the oranges to macerate at room temperature for a few hours before serving.

Citrus zest

It is unlikely that oranges or lemons will be waxed if you purchase them directly from a small producer at the local market. However, most commercial producers do wax their fruit to extend its shelf life Those same producers are extremely likely to have used a myriad of pesticides both before and after picking the fruit. So, when using the zest, which is packed with richly flavoured essential oils, be sure to buy fruit that is produced organically or labelled unwaxed. Otherwise, pour boiling water over the fruit and give it a light scrub before using.

Only use the outer skin of the fruit as the white pith is extremely bitter.

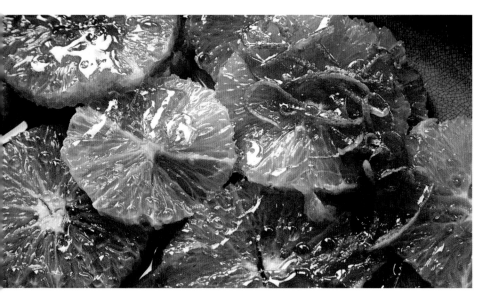

granizado de limón
lemon ice

Decades ago *Granizado de Limón* used to be sold from small carts on the streets of Valencia. The refreshing half-drink/half-sorbet was a wonderful antidote to the stifling summer heat before the days of air conditioning. Nowadays you can buy *Granizado* from bars the length of the Mediterranean coast, but sadly much of it is made from sickly commercial syrup. Once you taste the real thing you will know. This makes a refreshing afternoon drink or light dessert.

makes just over 600 ml/1 pint
3 lemons
6 tbsp caster sugar
1 litre/2 pints water

Using a potato peeler, pare the lemons. You just want the outer skin and none of the bitter pith.

Place the lemon peel, sugar and 150 ml/5 fl oz water in a pan and simmer for 5 minutes. Strain the lemon syrup and add the remaining water and the juice of the lemons. Pour the mixture into a shallow container and freeze.

As the *granizado* begins to harden, remove from the freezer and stir with a fork. Repeat this process 3 times. Serve while still slushy or you can leave it to defrost slightly before serving.

Alternatively, if you have a sturdy blender, freeze the *granizado* in ice-cube trays – you can always store the cubes in a bag once frozen – then whiz the cubes to a slush before serving in tall glasses.

Tip   You could leave the freezing out altogether and serve this as refreshing lemonade with a few fresh mint leaves and an ice cube.

The indispensable fruit
Lemons are vital in the Spanish kitchen. The zest flavours countless desserts but more importantly the juice is used as a last minute seasoning for many a savoury dish, adding a zippy, fresh touch. So, when you season your food don't just consider that familiar duo of salt and pepper but lemon juice and extra virgin olive oil too.
   A whole lemon studded with cloves makes an excellent fridge freshener and is also reputed to keep away flies, should you be cooking or eating out of doors.

tarta de manzana
apple cake

Apple orchards clothe many of the lush hillsides of the North, from Asturias to the Basque country. Admittedly much of the crop is destined for cider: a local passion. From January to April the Basques flock to the *Sagardotegiak*, cider houses, to down the new season brew, fresh from the barrel. Meanwhile, Asturian barmen pour their cider from an arm's length above the head into a glass clasped at the thigh – a deft feat of showmanship that aerates the otherwise flat cider. Thankfully some apples do escape the press; table varieties such as the *Reineta*, or Russet, make delicious eating.

Cooking with apples
Reineta, or Russet, Golden Delicious and Granny Smith are the ideal apples to cook with as they hold their shape well and also have a good flavour. They are all available in Spain.

Peeled apples turn brown in a trice, so always dip in lemon juice or prepare a bowl of water with a little lemon juice to place them in while preparing your dish. Drain and dry off before use.

serves 8–10

- 170 g/6 oz butter, softened, plus extra for greasing
- 3 eating apples, peeled and sliced
- ½ tsp ground cinnamon
- 1 tsp vanilla extract
- juice of ½ lemon
- 3 tbsp cider
- 170 g/6 oz soft brown sugar, or a mixture of dark brown sugar and caster sugar
- 3 eggs, beaten
- 170 g/6 oz flour
- 2 tsp baking powder

for the glaze
- 2 tbsp lemon juice
- 3 tbsp icing sugar

Preheat the oven to 190°C/375°F/Gas Mark 5.

Grease a 23 cm/9 inch springform cake tin with butter and line the base with baking paper.

Toss the apples with the cinnamon, vanilla extract, lemon juice and cider. In another bowl, beat the butter and sugar together until light and fluffy. Gradually add the egg to the butter and sugar a little at a time. Take care to beat thoroughly between additions, throwing in a tablespoon of flour if the mixture begins to curdle.

Strain off the liquid from the apple slices. Sift the flour and baking powder together and fold into the cake mixture together with the liquid from the apple slices.

Now spread the mixture over the base of the prepared tin and add the apple slices. You need not be too precious about the arrangement, as the sponge will rise up and cover most of the apple. Place in the middle of the oven and cook for about 50 minutes until a deep, golden brown colour. Spear the centre of the cake with a skewer, it should come out clean, any 'custardy' juices mean the cake needs a few more minutes. Leave the cake to cool slightly in the tin.

Meanwhile, mix together the lemon juice and icing sugar to make a thin glaze. Brush the top of the cake with the glaze and serve warm or at room temperature.

manzanas al horno
baked apples

These apples are an autumnal treat, stuffed with whatever mixture of dried fruit and nuts that comes to hand. It is an ideal opportunity to clear the baking cupboard of all the bags of stray ingredients before they are past their best. Alternatively, you may go to the market and find the *puesto de frutos secos* – an entire stall devoted to dried fruit and nuts, and buy a wonderful selection specifically for the dish.

serves 4

30 g/1 oz butter, softened
8 dried apricots, dates or figs, or a mixture, roughly chopped
2 tbsp raisins or sultanas
4 tbsp dark rum, brandy or sweet sherry
4 *Reineta*, or other firm eating apples

3 tbsp chopped roasted almonds, hazelnuts, pine kernels or walnuts, or a mixture
90 g/3¼ oz brown sugar or 3 tbsp honey
ice cream, to serve

Preheat the oven to 190°C/375°F/Gas Mark 5.

Grease a small ovenproof dish with a little of the butter. Place the dried fruit and alcohol in a small pan and heat gently until piping hot. Or you can use the microwave. Leave the mixture to macerate.

Meanwhile, remove the cores from the apples. You may have a gadget for the job, but a bit of careful excavation with a small kitchen knife will work too. Next, using a sharp knife, cut an equator through the skin around each apple to prevent the apple from splitting during cooking. Place the apples in the prepared dish.

Mix the remaining butter, nuts, half of the sugar, the dried fruit and alcohol together and stuff the apples with the mixture. Top with the remaining sugar or honey.

Pour about 1 cm/½ inch of water around the apples and bake for about 45 minutes, or until tender. Serve warm with any escaped juices and a spoonful of ice cream.

Variations   For an ambrosial dessert you could bake empty, cored apples until tender then, while still warm, fill with *Crema Catalana* custard (see page 119). Top with plenty of sugar and then place under the grill to brown. Serve right away.

Incorporate 150 g/5 oz of minced pork together with a pinch of ground cinnamon into the stuffing, substitute the rum with white wine and you have Catalan *pomes farcides*, a traditional *fiesta* favourite.

compota de cerezas
cherry compote

Extremadura is cherry country, and in June the weekly markets in Cáceres and Plasencia are inundated with the fruit. Entire stalls sell the magenta, heart-shaped *picotas*, a highly esteemed local variety. The nearby valley of Jerte is Europe's largest cherry orchard. Village doorways hang with hand-written signs '*hay cerezas*', cherries for sale, and the fruit is distilled to make a potent brandy, *aguardiente*.

Lusciously ripe cherries are a treat just as they come, but this simple recipe makes a fabulous change. Try stirring the compote into yogurt or cream, whiz with ice cream for a few seconds in a food processor for a cheat's cherry ripple, or serve with almond meringues (see *Soplillos* on page 122).

serves 8

450 g/1 lb ripe cherries, stoned
150 g/5 oz brown sugar
100 ml/3¹/₂ fl oz water

100 ml/3¹/₂ fl oz *aguardiente de cereza*, the local cherry 'firewater', or Kirsch

Place the cherries in a non-reactive pan, stainless steel or enamel will do fine, with the sugar, alcohol and water. Simmer gently for 40 minutes, stirring from time to time.

If the compote seems very runny, then strain the cherries, place the syrup back in the pan and boil until reduced. Leave to cool and serve as required.

Buying and storing cherries
Select firm and shiny fruit with its green stem still intact.

Colour is nothing to go by as fabulously sweet cherries can range from pale peachy shades right through to purple depending on the variety.

Do ask for a taste; cherries must be picked when fully ripe since their sugar levels will not increase in the fruit bowl.

Keep cherries in the refrigerator in hot weather, but do not wash or remove stalks until the last minute. *Guindas* are very sour cherries, which are ideal for cooking, but inedible raw, while *cerezas* are their sweeter cousins.

gratinado de higo
fig and sherry gratin

A lusciously ripe fig needs no accompaniment at all, but if you are lucky, you may just find yourself with a glut of fruit. This dessert is an absolute treat – a *zabaglione* with a Spanish sherry twist. You could add some raspberries or blackberries too.

serves 4

8 ripe figs
a pinch of ground cinnamon
4 egg yolks

100 g/4 oz caster sugar
70 ml/2½ fl oz *Oloroso* sherry

Slice the figs thinly. There is no need to peel them unless the skin feels particularly tough. Arrange the figs in a heatproof serving dish or 4 individual *Crema Catalana* dishes and sprinkle with cinnamon.

Next place the egg yolks, sugar and sherry in a heatproof bowl set over a pan of boiling water and whisk together until you have a luxuriously creamy, light foam. Reduce the heat and continue beating until the mixture is thick and pale.

Pour the mixture over the figs and refrigerate until almost ready to serve or, alternatively, go to the next step straightaway.

Heat the grill to its highest setting and place the figs under the heat until the egg mixture begins to brown. Serve at once.

Sweet and savoury
The natural sweetness of a ripe fig is fabulous paired with *jamón, sobrasada* (see page 49) or salty, blue cheese such as Picos de Europa.

Figs also seem to have a natural affinity with duck. Try warming a few in the oven with a dash of brandy and serving alongside a pink duck breast.

Buying and storing figs
Figs have two seasons in Spain. The first to arrive, in early summer, are the bigger *brevas*. Many favour these over the late summer *higos*, saying that they are more flavoursome and thinner skinned. I love both.

There is no general rule that a green fig should be tastier than a black one, they are purely different varieties, although the most highly prized Spanish fig is the green '*cuello de dama*' from Tiétar valley to the west of Madrid.

At the market it is advisable to select figs that are still just firm or you will end up with something resembling 'road kill' by the time you get home.

Leave the figs to ripen on a windowsill or patio and eat while still warm from the sun. Ripe figs will begin to ooze a juicy nectar, the *miel de higo*, from their base. A slightly firmer fig will benefit enormously from a few minutes in a medium-hot oven to warm through.

fresas con vinagre
strawberries with vinegar

Spanish strawberries can range from rather disappointing, monstrous things the size of an apricot, grown out of season, under acres of polythene in the South, to the petite and delectable Catalan *Maduixes del Maresme*. The latter are grown on the slopes of the Mediterranean Maresme coast to the north of Barcelona. In spring the locals are prepared to pay premium prices to enjoy their unbeatable flavour and would possibly consider the vinegar treatment absolute heresy. Thankfully there are abundant supplies of well-priced sun-ripened strawberries all over Spain in spring and early summer, so you may like to give this a try.

serves 4

450 g/1 lb strawberries, hulled and halved
1–2 tbsp caster sugar to taste
½–1 tbsp mature sherry vinegar

First you will need to gauge the sweetness and acidity of your ingredients – a perfectly good excuse to tuck in to a few strawberries while you are working.

If the strawberries are beautifully ripe and sweet you may decide to add less sugar. It is worth tasting the vinegar too, some of the more matured varieties are rich and mellow while others are quite acidic; just adjust the quantity according to taste.

Leave the fruit to macerate for at least 2 hours in the refrigerator. Allow to reach room temperature while you eat the rest of your meal and serve with *Nata Montada*, or whipped cream with a pinch of sugar.

sandía con hierbabuena
watermelon with mint

'A watermelon is like a marriage; you have no idea what it will be like until you take the plunge,' said the lady at the melon stall with a mischievous grin. And so, after years of knowledgeable tapping and listening for hollow clues, it turns out that it is all just down to potluck.

serves 4

4 large slices of watermelon
8 fresh mint leaves, finely chopped

Cut the fruit into small triangles, or balls if you must, then remove as many seeds as possible and stir up with a touch of mint before serving.

Tips This makes a really refreshing lunchtime dessert, as watermelon is a great natural thirst quencher. Or, for a touch of sophistication you could try serving this as a palate cleanser between courses.

You can, of course, add a little caster sugar if the watermelon is not quite sweet enough. 150g/5 oz stoned cherries would make a delicious addition too.

melocotones al vino rosado
rosé poached peaches

The Lérida province of Catalonia is home to vast orchards and olive groves and so every Saturday Balaguer's arcaded square is transformed into a bustling market of fabulous local produce. The archways afford some shade and protection from the searing sun, but still the perfume of ripe peaches warmed by the all-pervasive heat is unforgettable.

serves 4

6 ripe peaches, skinned (see tip)
1 bottle rosé wine
5 tbsp caster sugar
1 vanilla pod, split in half
  lengthways
2 large peelings of lemon zest

Halve the peaches and carefully remove the stones.

Pour the wine into a large pan that will accommodate all your peaches and add the sugar, vanilla pod and lemon zest. Add the peaches together with just enough water to cover them and bring to the boil. Reduce the heat and simmer for about 15 minutes. Remove the peaches from the wine syrup and set aside.

Now boil the wine syrup until it reduces to a thick, sticky syrup. Remove the vanilla pod and lemon zest. Serve the peaches covered in the fabulously aromatic syrup.

Tip   To skin truly ripe peaches, you can cover them with boiling water for about 30 seconds. The skin should slip off easily rather like a tomato skin. Firmer fruit will need to be simmered for 3–4 minutes until the skins slide off.

peras al vino tinto
red wine-poached pears

The length of time that you poach these pears will be down to the ripeness of the fruit. Ideally the flesh should yield a little around the stem when pinched. You may prefer to leave the pears whole, in which case, you should add 10 minutes to the poaching time.

serves 4

1 bottle young red wine
4 tbsp caster sugar
1 stick cinnamon
zest and juice of 1 orange
6 ripe pears, peeled, cored and
  halved

Place the wine, sugar, cinnamon and orange zest and juice in a large pan that is big enough to accommodate all the pears. Add the pears together with just enough water to cover them and simmer for 15 minutes, or until the flesh seems tender rather than soft. Remove the pears to serving dish and set aside.

Now boil the poaching liquid until it reduces by two-thirds to a sticky syrup. Serve hot or cold, depending on the season, poured over the pears.

dulce de membrillo
quince paste

Quinces make a timely arrival in autumn when luscious peaches, cherries and soft fruits are long gone and the citrus season has yet to begin in earnest. Keen Spanish cooks snap up the fragrant fruit and busy themselves making jelly to last the winter while many of us would not give the quince a second glance.

It is certainly no conventional beauty, resembling a large ungainly pear with the odd patch of grey down. It hardly screams 'buy me'. It is not convenience food either since its flesh is virtually inedible raw. Yet, with a little cooking and a spoonful of sugar (or ten!) the fruit is transformed into a rusty red delight, with its own honeyed flavour and deliciously granular texture. *Dulce de Membrillo* makes a wonderful partner for sharp cheeses and keeps for months.

makes a large slab

1 kg/2¼ lb quinces, washed but not peeled

about 300 ml/10 fl oz water

about 750 g/1½ lb caster sugar (see method)

Wipe away any suede-like down from the quince skin, remove the cores and cut the fruit into chunks. The flesh will discolour as it oxidizes, but it is not a problem as your jelly will be a rich reddish brown by the time you have finished.

Place the quinces in a large pan with the water, bring to the boil and cook until it softens, about 20–30 minutes, then strain off the water.

Now you need to purée the fruit. Ideally you would use a *pasapurés* (see page 17), because this will leave the pulp skin-free, but you can whiz in a food processor, then strain the purée through a very fine sieve or muslin.

Weigh the purée and add an equal weight of sugar. Return to the pan and simmer gently until the sugar has dissolved. Increase the heat and boil until the mixture thickens. This will probably take at least an hour of regular stirring. Beware – the paste will spit like the devil, so use your longest wooden spoon and an oven-glove. Eventually, and patience is required, the paste will turn a deep, brick red colour and the spoon will virtually stand up by itself.

Line a small tin with greaseproof paper. The shape is up to you, but a loaf tin would do nicely. Fill with the paste and leave to set for a minimum of 12 hours.

Once the paste has set you can turn it out onto a board. Wrap in clingfilm and store in a cool place.

Variation   *Dulce de Membrillo* is fabulous served with lamb, when combined with garlic and extra virgin olive oil in a mortar, or food processor.

Tennis elbow?
Or just lacking time and inclination for all that stirring:
The paste can be cooked in the microwave with excellent results.

Once you have mixed together the quince purée and sugar place it in a roomy glass bowl; you must leave plenty of space for expansion. Cover with microwave clingfilm and cook on the medium setting for 15 minutes.

Remove from the microwave with extreme care – you are dealing with molten lava, and give the paste a stir. Re-cover and repeat the process twice more until the paste is wonderfully thick and turns a deep brick red colour.

Microwave settings do vary, so if the jelly seems pale and syrupy you may need to give it one last 10 minute blast.

macedonia de otoño
autumnal fruit salad

Sweet potato may seem a bizarre addition to this seasonal fruit salad, but this is not some fanciful experiment, *boniato* is used in many traditional Spanish sweets. Small *empanada* pastries are filled with sweet potato in Valencia, while fried slices are served with honey in Mallorca.

serves 6–8
juice of 1 lemon
3 tbsp honey
about 300 ml/10 fl oz hot water
1 stick cinnamon
500 g/1 lb 2 oz quinces
500 g/1 lb 2 oz sweet potatoes, ideally the orange fleshed variety, washed but not peeled

6 oranges, 4 peeled, cut into pith-free slices/segments, and 2 juiced
2 apples, cut into small chunks and dipped in the orange juice
juice of ½ lemon (optional)
1–2 tbsp honey (optional)

to serve
2 tbsp toasted flaked almonds
yogurt or cream

Preheat the oven to 180°C/350°F/Gas Mark 4.

Mix the lemon juice, honey and the hot water together, then pour the liquid into a baking tin or ovenproof dish large enough to fit the quince halves in a single layer.

Cut the quinces in half and remove the stalks and cores. The fruit will be very hard so a good paring knife will come in handy. A sharp melon-baller is great for removing the core too. Place the quinces, cut-side down, in the tin or dish before they have a chance to brown. Add the cinnamon and bake for until tender, about 30 minutes to 1 hour. Make sure all the liquid does not evaporate and the quinces burn while baking, so top up the liquid, if necessary – this will make a delicious syrup.

Leave the quinces to cool, then cut into small chunks. You may like to remove the peel, but that is up to you. Reserve the syrup left in the tin, ideally about 150 ml/5 fl oz. If you have a lot more syrup then you could boil it for a moment or two to reduce down.

Meanwhile, prick the sweet potatoes and bake them for 20–40 minutes, depending on size, until just tender. Leave to cool, then peel off the skin and cut into small chunks.

Place the quinces, potatoes, oranges and apples in a large serving bowl.

Mix the orange juice and quince syrup together and pour over the fruit. Taste – too sweet, add the lemon juice, too tart and a little honey will do the trick.

Serve at room temperature sprinkled with flaked almonds and accompanied by yogurt or cream.

Variation   The quinces make a glorious dessert by themselves. Allow half a quince per person and serve cut-side up with the fragrant cooking syrup and large dollop of yogurt mixed with honey.

Buying, storing and preparing quinces

A ripe quince is rock hard, if the flesh is soft it is probably rotten. Avoid blemished fruit although the customary suede-like grey patches on the skin are not a problem.

Golden fruit are ideal for baking and poaching in sweet or savoury dishes while the less ripe, greenish-yellow fruit are higher in pectin and perfect for the thick setting *Dulce de Membrillo* opposite.

Once home, place the quinces in a fruit bowl allowing them to fill the kitchen with their glorious scent. Quinces will keep in the refrigerator for about a month, but do be sure to wrap them or their pervasive fragrance will taint the entire contents of the refrigerator.

Peeled fruit will oxidize and brown unless you dip it in citrus juice or acidulated water. It is not usually a problem since cooked quince gains a glorious terracotta hue in any case, particularly when combined with sugar.

Poach quince with a little sugar until tender, from about 20 minutes to an hour, and add to casseroles such as the lamb shanks on page 62 (omitting the olives). Baked quince is also delicious (see left).

ensalada de granadas y escarola
pomegranate and curly endive salad

It is no coincidence that Granada, Spain's last Moorish bastion, was named after this sensual fruit since it was the Arabs who first introduced the pomegranate from Persia. Piles of exotic looking pomegranates make a wonderful spectacle in winter markets. They are invariably topped with a few alluring samples, sliced open to reveal their magenta, jewel-like seeds.

serves 4

2 pomegranates, seeds and juice reserved (see right)
salt and freshly ground black pepper
1 curly endive, washed and ripped into small pieces

2 red peppers, roasted, peeled (see page 144) and cut into ribbons

for the dressing
juice of 1 lemon
1 tsp French mustard
3 tbsp extra virgin olive oil

Mix the dressing ingredients together with any pomegranate juice and season with salt and pepper to taste.

Place the endive, pepper ribbons and half the pomegranate seeds together in a large bowl and toss with the dressing. Sprinkle with the remaining seeds and serve.

Buying and storing
A ripe pomegranate should feel heavy and sound almost metallic when tapped. Avoid any fruit with cracked skin that may be overripe and will soon turn bad. The colour of the pomegranate will depend on the variety – from mottled pale pink to deep red. I find that the darker fruit have consistently darker seeds that look the most dramatic as a garnish. Pomegranates benefit from a few days storage at room temperature as they become increasingly juicy and flavoursome.

Releasing the seeds
Place a sieve over a small bowl. Cut the pomegranate around its equator and give the halves a good squeeze over the sieve to loosen the seeds. Now tap the outside of the pomegranate with a spoon, allowing the juice and seeds to fall into the sieve. Make sure to throw away any white pith – it is terribly bitter.
    Pomegranate juice stains, so make sure you wear an apron for this job.

index

174

acknowledgements

Huge thanks:

To Peter – this book would have been impossible without your incredible enthusiasm and dedication. Thank you for accompanying me on the months of research, for taking wonderful photographs, for remaining the chilled chauffeur (most of the time) with the worst navigator yet, for walking the streets of Bristol with little Mrs Mimms so that I could get the writing done and just for always being there.

To all my family, especially Mum, for their great support and encouragement.

To everyone at Books for Cooks and Divertimenti, I haven't forgotten you all, I just got waylaid in a sea of purées and prams.

To all my wonderful friends in Bristol for being such eager guinea pigs and to Gill, Genevieve and Clare for your patience and cooking skills.

To my Grandparents in Ibiza and the Nicolau family in Castellón, who ignited my insatiable passion for Spain.

To Spanish friends who made the research a delight: to Cheche, Gabriel and the rest of the Cirera family, to Mercè and Jaume and everyone at El Folló, to Marta and Ramón, to Yolanda and Juan, to Fernando and his niece Eva, to Rafael in the Alpujarras and Pilar in Miranda.

To all the wonderfully generous stall holders and shoppers in the Spanish markets who were so happy to share their recipes, tips and experiences with me. They created this book.

To the entire team at Anova Books: to Kate Oldfield for getting the wheels turning and to Anna Cheifetz for being so understanding about the time constraints of writing with a new baby around. To Emily Preece-Morrison for always being so calm and supportive and for miraculously tailoring my lengthy text to fit the pages and to Kathy Steer for her painstaking copy-editing.

To Vanessa Courtier for bringing the book to life with fabulous pictures and stunning design, to Janie Suthering for getting up at 5 am and making the food look so delicious and to Wei Tang for her beautifully natural styling.